The Case for Ve...

The Case for Vegetarianism

Philosophy for a Small Planet

John Lawrence Hill

Rowman & Littlefield Publishers, Inc.

ROWMAN & LITTLEFIELD PUBLISHERS, INC.

Published in the United States of America
by Rowman & Littlefield Publishers, Inc.
4720 Boston Way, Lanham, Maryland 20706

3 Henrietta Street
London, WC2E 8LU, England

British Cataloging in Publication Information Available

Library of Congress Cataloging-in-Publication Data

Hill, John L. (John Lawrence).
The case for vegetarianism : philosophy for a small planet / John
Lawrence Hill.
p.   cm.
Includes bibliographical references and index.
1. Vegetarianism.   I. Title.
TX392.H528   1996   613.2'62—dc20   95–26192   CIP

ISBN 0–8476–8137–8   (cloth : alk. paper)
ISBN 0–8476–8138–6   (pbk. : alk. paper)

Printed in the United States of America

∞™ The paper used in this publication meets the minimum requirements of
American National Standard for Information Sciences—Permanence of
Paper for Printed Library Materials, ANSI Z39.48–1984.

Dedication
To Ananda, my daughter, my bliss.

Contents

Introduction

Over the course of the last two decades, social awareness has turned increasingly to the issue of animal rights, with particular emphasis on the the use of animals in medical experimentation. For example, should animals be sacrificed in large numbers so that humans might have a cure for cancer? To develop remedies for less-serious conditions, such as allergies? What about the development of a new brand of lipstick? Various thinkers have drawn lines in diverse places with results ranging from pan-species egalitarianism at one end of the spectrum to unabashed claims for the absolute priority of human interests at the other, and with a wide variety of more "pragmatic" and "moderate" positions between these two polar extremes. As significant as these ethical and social issues are, however, the outcry over animal experimentation has served to overshadow a profoundly more important issue: the question of the wholesale slaughter of animals for human consumption.

Estimates of the number of animals used in various experimental settings nationwide and around the world vary. In the United States each year, somewhere between 20 and 70 million laboratory animals are used for commercial, medical, and scientific purposes, though some estimates place the number as high as 100 million. Worldwide, roughly 225 million animals are similarly used. About 90 percent of these are rodents, while dogs, cats, and other higher mammals make up a large portion of the remainder. Perhaps a quarter of these are used in medical research, strictly speaking, while the remainder are used in commercial toxicity testing, institutional uses in schools and universities, and other non-medical contexts.[1]

While these numbers are astronomical, they pale in comparison with the use of animals for human consumption. In the United States alone, each year people eat 3.3 billion broiler chickens, 85 million pigs, 112 million beef cattle, and 9 million sheep.[2] In his or her lifetime, the average American consumes 11 cattle, 1 calf, 3 lambs and sheep, 23 hogs, 45 turkeys, 1,100 chicken, and 862 pounds of fish, for a total of about two hundred pounds of meat per year and over seven tons of meat in a lifetime.[3]

Whatever one may think about the case against animal experimentation, the case against eating meat is abundantly more compelling for three reasons. First, the numbers themselves indicate that the exploitation and destruction of animals in experimental settings is marginal compared to the ravages of meat eating. To take one example, in the United States the number of pigs consumed by humans each year exceeds the total number of animals "sacrificed" in experimental settings. Thus, even if we ignore the use for human consumption of all other species and discount the mental capacity of domestic pigs, who are easily as intelligent and good-natured as dogs, the habit of meat eating presents a moral issue equally compelling to that of experimentation on animals. Indeed, it is estimated that in the United States even a 1 percent increase in the number of humans adhering to a vegetarian diet would have the same effect in the reduction of animal suffering as would the total abolition of all forms of animal experimentation.[4]

Second, unlike the issue of animal experimentation, where at least a *prima facie* case can be made for the need for such experimentation in medical contexts, there is no conflict between human well-being and the vegetarian diet. Quite the reverse is true. The switch to vegetarianism is in our own best interest. From the standpoint of physical or mental health as well as from an ecological perspective, vegetarianism is an eminently practical—if not downright necessary—regimen.

Finally, in contrast to the relatively more indirect methods of bringing about the curtailment or outright abolition of animal experimentation (e.g., protests, lobbying, and similar activities), becoming a vegetarian is the most direct way of evincing one's commitment to the doctrine of nonviolence to animals and to one's own good health. With a reduction in the demand for meat goes the suffering and exploitation of animals.

The Demographics of Vegetarianism

Roughly nine million Americans, or about 4 percent of the total population, consider themselves to be vegetarians.[5] Although the group is as yet small in proportion to the larger population, it is unexpectedly diverse demographically. According to one recent survey, 40 percent hold professional or managerial occupations, 24 percent are blue-collar workers, 16 percent are students, 12 percent are homemakers, and another 9 percent are employed in clerical or sales positions. Women make up 71 percent and 29 percent are men. The median age of all vegetarians is thirty-five. Nor is abstinence from meat a passing fad for most who adopt the vegetarian lifestyle. The median length of time that those surveyed had been vegetarians was eight years.[6]

The reasons people become vegetarians are equally varied. With some overlap, 67 percent were concerned with animal suffering, 38 percent were primarily motivated by considerations of health, 17 percent were moved by religious reasons, with a smattering of such other motives as a distaste for meat (12 percent), personal growth (7 percent), concern about world hunger (5 percent), and economic reasons (3 percent). Of this same group, 38 percent were motivated purely by ethical and social concerns, 19 percent for health reasons, and 43 percent became vegetarians for a combination of reasons.[7] This plurality of motives for becoming vegetarian attests not only to the diversity of vegetarians themselves, but to the fact that the case for vegetarianism can be made equally on altruistic and egoistic grounds.

Many of the greatest minds in history have personally endorsed vegetarianism. To list these names is not to engage in the fallacy of appeal to authority, to argue that vegetarianism is *ipso facto* morally preferable simply because certain authorities have said so. Rather, the list is included to suggest that some of the most profound thinkers, scientists, and artists of the ages have resisted conforming to the sometimes overwhelming culture of meat consumption. Adherence to vegetarianism has often come as the result of calm reflection upon the evils of needless animal sacrifice; in other cases, it has resulted from what can only be described as a kind of spiritual awakening, the recognition that pain and suffering are experienced by all sentient creatures, not just human beings.

From the earliest times, the Greek scientist, mathematician, and philosopher Pythagoras was a staunch vegetarian. The father of ancient rationalism and humanism, Socrates, is also reported to have been a vegetarian. His student, Plato, advocated vegetarianism as the best diet suited to the ideal society in *The Republic*; Plato in turn may have influenced Aristotle's similar dietary predilections. The Roman poet Ovid and philosopher and orator Seneca were also vegetarians. Among Christian thinkers, St. Jerome and St. Benedict were vegetarians, as was the founder of modern Methodism, John Wesley. (See chapter 2 for a discussion regarding the ambivalent Christian attitude toward animal slaughter for human consumption.)

In the modern era, Leonardo da Vinci, Isaac Newton, Voltaire, Benjamin Franklin, Henry David Thoreau, Leo Tolstoy, Thomas Edison, George Bernard Shaw, Albert Schweitzer, and Mahatma Gandhi were vegetarians.[8] The assembled achievements of this group, morally, politically, artistically, philosophically and scientifically suggest minimally that moral vision may at least sometimes accompany intellectual greatness; their converse, conformity and mediocrity, are all too regular bedfellows.

Overview of the Book

The Case for Vegetarianism is written both for nonphilosophers and for students of philosophy. It is intended to say something both about philosophy, particularly applied moral philosophy, and about the argument for vegetarianism. As such, Janus-faced, the book looks in two directions simultaneously—to the continued power and relevance of philosophical thought as a method unto itself and to its application in the "real world."

Aristotle distinguished humankind from the rest of the animal kingdom by calling us "the rational animal." With some mild embarrassment, and notwithstanding the modern intellectual assaults on our pretensions to rationality from Freudians, existentialists, social deconstructionists, and others, we still cling, sometimes desperately, to this image. It is, after all, about the only thing we have that still serves to distinguish us from our relatives in the animal kingdom and even this, as I shall argue in chapter 2, has been greatly exaggerated.

But if anything remains of the bastion of rationality and of the notion that there are genuine moral obligations to other beings, the case for vegetarianism is convincing. In short, if nothing really matters such that all our behavior occurs in a great moral vacuum, and if we act only from convenience or passion or the will to power, then no argument can ever suffice to convince a person to change his or her outlook or behavior. If, on the other hand, there remains a shred of something objective—something outside ourselves—that *matters* and if the moral universe has not completely fallen in upon itself, compressed to a point where that point is me (or you in your moral universe), then, if ever a case can be made, it can be made for vegetarianism. Whether the reasons are those having to do with the rights or interests of other species, the self-interested argument from one's own health, the destruction done to the environment by the human consumption of animals, the possibility of feeding the starving millions around the globe, or some combination thereof, the answer is the same: the case for vegetarianism is absolutely compelling.

In chapter 1, "The Traditional Roots of Modern Moral Philosophy and the Case for Vegetarianism," I lay out in broad strokes the reasons for the need for philosophical argument in the first place. Then I sketch the three great traditions in moral philosophy: virtue ethics, deontology, and utilitarianism. This is done both to give the reader a working familiarity with philosophical thought and to pave the way for arguments that will be considered subsequently in the book. No great degree of abstract, technical precision is sought here and this overview will be, of necessity, brief, general—an overview. However, the general contours of these philosophical traditions and arguments will be sketched so that the reader leaves with a sound understanding as to how these traditions and arguments play out in the context of the case for vegetarianism. The reader who is primarily interested in vegetarianism, with less interest in moral thought as such, may wish to begin directly with chapter 2.

In chapter 2, "The Argument from the Rights and Interests of Animals," we will examine the case for animal rights, most broadly construed. The chapter will begin with a discussion of religious, particularly Christian, attitudes regarding the moral status of animals. Then we will consider the utilitarian and deontological approaches to the rights and interests of animals. As we shall see, the utilitarian case for animal protection focuses largely upon the pain caused to animals by modern methods of livestock production and by animal slaughter, while deontological arguments are predicated upon animals' status as beings worthy of moral consideration. One question that I will seek to answer here is whether animals have the same moral status as human beings and, if not, whether vegetarianism should be morally obligatory at all. A significant portion of the chapter will also be devoted to a discussion of the mental states of animals. I will argue that some animals, particularly higher mammals, do in fact think, feel, and even act as moral agents, making decisions and carrying them out (often in aid of humans or other animals). Finally, the chapter will conclude with a consideration of the relative interests of animals, infants, and the mentally handicapped and the status of each in light of their relative intellectual capacities.

In chapter 3, "The Argument from Personal Health," we will examine some of the traditional arguments made against vegetarianism, which are based on the supposed similarity of humans and carnivores. We will consider similar arguments on the other side, all of which have a decidedly "natural law" tinge to them. Then we will look at some of the specific (and dangerous) consequences to health inherent in meat eating, along with a discussion of the physical benefits of the vegetarian diet. The discussion will also include a consideration of the connection between vegetarianism, optimum mental health and virtue ethics.

In chapter 4, "The Argument from Global Ecology," we turn to a consideration of the disastrous ecological consequences of modern meat production, including deforestation, land erosion and desertification, and water and air pollution, among others. We will also discuss the changing focus of morality in the modern world from the internalized, otherworldly Christian ethic to the recent transition and demand that our moral imperatives extend to other species and world ecology at large.

As implied by the title to chapter 5, "The Argument from World Hunger," here we will examine the claim that famine, both at home and abroad, could be abated, even eliminated, by adopting a vegetarian diet. The chapter will investigate the causes of world hunger and will explore the connection between meat production and the maldistribution of food worldwide.

Chapter 6, "Some Objections to Vegetarianism Considered," is interesting both as a resource guide to the beleaguered vegetarian under attack from his or her meat-eating friends and associates, and as an overview of some of the more common logical fallacies employed in defense of meat eating. The chapter will consider the claim that meat eating is actually good for animals because it ensures that greater numbers of animals will be born than would be true if everyone were vegetarian, the argument that vegetarians are inconsistent because they still eat plants, the assertion that meat eating is "natural" for human beings, and a number of other objections to vegetarianism.

Chapter 7, "Vegetarianism and Moral Progress," concludes this study by discussing the underlying social and moral question: How can vegetarians be so certain they are correct when the great majority of people do not share their convictions? The chapter argues, most fundamentally, that inherent in the concept of moral progress is the idea that later generations come to accept and embrace ideas that are unpopular, even unthinkable, by earlier generations. The protection of all sentient life may be one such emerging moral conviction.

Chapter One

The Traditional Roots of
Modern Moral Philosophy and
the Case for Vegetarianism

In the fourth century B.C., there lived in Greece a philosopher later known as Diogenes the Cynic. Diogenes was known for his pranks, his flaunting of convention, and his distrust both for academic philosophy and for systematic attempts to arrive at objective knowledge of the world through argument or analysis. So averse was Diogenes to the seemingly incessant ramblings of the other philosophers of his day and to their claims to wisdom that he regularly employed his considerable ingenuity at undermining and humiliating these other lesser minds.

Legend has it that one day Diogenes overheard a group of philosophers arguing in a courtyard behind a large wall. The philosophers were debating the definition of "man" and had decided that Aristotle's definition of man as "a rational animal" would have to be replaced as people were too seldom rational to justify the definition. As Diogenes listened, the group settled upon a new definition. Man was essentially, they decided, "a feather-less biped." At hearing this, Diogenes went to a nearby butcher shop, procured a plucked chicken, and returned to the scene where he threw the chicken over the wall and into the midst of the group proclaiming, "There is your featherless biped!"

There is nothing new about mistrust, and often even distrust, of the process of rational argument as a means to arriving at fundamental conclusions about the order of the cosmos, our purpose here on this earth, and the nature of our moral obligations to other persons, to other creatures, and to the world at large. This is perhaps partly because rational argument leads to con-

1

clusions we find difficult to accept intellectually. To paraphrase the philosopher Bertrand Russell, philosophy is the process by which we begin with undeniable premises and argue by flawless logic to unbelievable conclusions.

There is perhaps another more important reason we are sometimes skeptical of philosophical argument. Often, it appears, we are uncomfortable with the conclusions with which philosophy confronts us. Philosophy tests both our worldview and our moral courage to act in conformity with our intellectual principles. This is nowhere more true than in the realm of moral philosophy. The slaveholder confronted with the conclusion that owning slaves is morally unjust, or the racist, the sexist, and the xenophobe confronted with the proposition that it is wrong to discriminate against those of other races, sexes, or countries, finds one avenue of reaction by simply rejecting the conclusion along with the process that has generated it. Perhaps we all do this in our own small ways. Even the usually well-meaning rationalize fudging on their tax returns, telling white lies, or breaking promises deemed to be "insignificant." We do so in reaction to ideas and arguments we take none-too-seriously at other times.

Philosophy, then, can sometimes be a painful process, at least to the extent one seeks to live in conformity with one's conclusions. More often, however, philosophy is a liberating experience. If the truth does indeed set us free, then the road to truth is a quest for intellectual realization. And with intellectual realization comes freedom in the most significant sense of the word.

In this chapter, we will discuss the broad approaches to moral thought in our western tradition. Here we will discuss only tangentially the application of moral philosophy to vegetarianism.

The Quest for the Right Answer:
Moral Relativism versus Moral Realism

When people have "moral disagreements," what can philosophy do to help resolve the differences, to demonstrate which side is correct and which side is not? Minimally, what can philosophical interchange and argument do to find some common ground between disparate conclusions? Underlying these questions are issues of absolute significance to our entire sense of what morality is and what it requires.

Perhaps the most significant of these questions is whether there is, in the first place, an *objective sense* in which some actions are right and others wrong. To put it another way, is a moral statement a kind of factual statement? For example, is the statement "Murder is morally wrong" true in the same sense that the scientific statement "Water freezes at thirty-two degrees" or even the prosaic statement "I have five fingers on my left hand" are true?

Broadly speaking, there are two major positions one can take on this issue. One can be either a "moral realist" or a "moral relativist." Moral realists are people who believe that there are definite "rights" and "wrongs" in the world and that moral propositions such as "murder is wrong" are true in roughly the same way other factual or scientific statements are true. Moral relativists, on the other hand, believe that moral statements are not objectively true. They are not "factual" statements in any proper sense at all. While there are many different versions of moral relativism, a position that has found widespread support among numerous contemporary philosophers, the position usually boils down to the idea either that moral statements are merely expressions of feelings or tastes about a matter, or that they are expressions of cultural practices that vary from society to society.

Those moral relativists who believe that moral statements are simply expressions of individual feelings about a matter are called "ethical emotivists" ("emotivist" because the moral statement is taken to be nothing but a statement of emotion). This position holds basically that to say "murder is wrong" is more an expression of (subjective) individual taste or preference than an (objective) expression of fact about the act of murder. In other words, for the ethical emotivist, to say "murder is wrong" is to say "I don't approve of murder," "murder makes me feel great anger and frustration," or even "I want to see anyone who murders punished severely." In other words, it is more like saying "vanilla ice cream is boring" (an expression of taste) than like saying "water freezes at thirty-two degrees" (an expression of fact).

Emotivists, of course, understand that people often hold their moral positions with great fervor and thus with much more emotion than they would in maintaining that they do not enjoy vanilla ice cream. The point, however, is that, for the emotivist, just as the statement "vanilla ice cream is boring" tells us a good deal about *my taste* and little about vanilla ice cream itself, so too, the statement "murder is wrong" does not tell us anything objective about the rightness or wrongness of murder. It is merely a way (often a very strong way) of saying I disapprove of murder. It is, in short, a statement about my preferences and not about murder itself.

Another form of ethical relativism is known as "cultural relativism." Cultural relativism, which was largely inspired by cross-cultural studies conducted by anthropologists of various societies throughout the world, holds that moral statements are merely expressions of cultural practices and that, just as practices vary from culture to culture, so too do moral beliefs. Thus, in Catholic Spain, abortion is generally considered morally wrong while in Communist China, it is often considered morally obligatory.

For the cultural relativist, certain acts are right or wrong only in the context of a wider set of cultural practices and beliefs. There is no extracultural standard to which we can appeal to determine whether a particular culture is right or wrong. Rightness and wrongness are social constructs only; where conflicts exist between the beliefs in different cultures, these must go unresolved. Thus, again, to say that murder is wrong is not really to say anything about murder in itself, but only that it is not approved in one society (and may be approved in another). In contrast, factual statements such as "water freezes at thirty-two degrees" or "the sun is ninety three million miles from earth" are true independently of who says them—that is, they are "objective."

To the modern reader, ethical relativism in its various forms appears as an attractive position. Moral relativism appeals to our recently achieved sentiments of moral skepticism, tolerance, and pluralism. People are entitled to disagree, we say, largely for three reasons. First, who can say who is right and who is wrong in the first place (moral skepticism)? Second, much of what was once considered a matter of morality (e.g., decisions concerning private sexuality) is now considered a matter of private choice

(tolerance). Third, we are not even certain what these terms—
right and wrong—mean anymore. So, the reasoning goes, why
not let different societies and even different persons conduct their
own lifestyle experiments and see whose scheme works out best
(pluralism).

However, moral relativism carries with it one absolutely and
fundamentally troubling implication for our moral life: if moral
relativism in any of its various genres is accurate, then the terms
"good" and "bad," "right" and "wrong" lose just about all of
their significance. For the emotivist, no one really has any rational ground for criticizing another's moral practices or beliefs.
This would be like criticizing someone for preferring chocolate
to vanilla ice cream. If it is all a matter of personal taste in the
end, then no one has any basis for trying to persuade anyone
else that one position is good, better, or best. There is no better
or worse, no moral goal; there are only empty choices in a moral vacuum.

Take any moral standard whatsoever; if emotivism is true, that
standard cannot be defended. Thus, the person who believes that
slavery is just and proper, that women should never have been
given the vote (or, indeed, that they should live in total subjugation), that racial prejudice is defensible, that capital punishment is warranted for even the most minor infractions, that
abortion should be prohibited under every circumstance (or that
it should be permitted for any reason and at any time in preg-
nancy whatsoever)—none of these positions is ultimately susceptible of criticism for the emotivist. Oh, you may not *like*
somebody who adopts one of these positions, but this is a matter of pure, brute taste; there is little you can say ultimately to
persuade them that they are wrong.

Similarly, the cultural relativist takes strong medicine for his
or her moral convictions, or lack thereof. He or she must accept
any social practice, no matter how outrageous, unjust, or outright brutal, as long as it is commonly accepted within the con-
fines of a particular society. He or she must accept that human
sacrifice is morally permissible in Aztec Mexico, among other
places. He or she must condone cannibalism in New Guinea and
wife burning in India. He or she must accept slavery in the antebellum South and the suppression of human rights in Commu-

nist China. He or she must also embrace, with the cold eye of
scientific objectivity and moral neutrality, the slaughter of the
Jews in Nazi Germany because, after all, this was the prevailing
practice in that society. Further, for the cultural relativist, the
reformer can *never* be right because, by definition, reformers seek
to change social standards and practices. Moral conservatism is
perhaps the most insidious of implications of cultural relativism.
Moral standards may change in any particular society but, for
the cultural relativist, no argument can be given to hasten such
change.

The modern moral mind is peculiarly schizophrenic on the
question of moral realism. The modern liberal wants to be a moral
realist when it comes to condemning racial injustice, discrimination, the subjugation of women, or the inequitable distribution
of wealth in our society and the world at large. But he also runs
for the shelter of moral relativism on issues such as the right to
an abortion, gay rights, or the right to use recreational drugs.
(This is not to suggest that these positions cannot be defended
on realist principles, but simply that they seldom are.) Conversely,
the modern conservative may proclaim the right to life of the
unborn fetus in tones of staunch realism and simultaneously defend the most recent example of American international adven-
turism on the relativistic grounds, roughly and rudely speaking,
that "might makes right."

What we must come to terms with is that we cannot have it
both ways. Either moral practices and beliefs are objective statements amenable to rational criticism or they are mere manifesta-
tions of feeling, taste, tradition, or some subconscious will to
power. If realism is true, then we must take seriously reasons
and arguments for taking one rather than another position. If, on
the other hand, one chooses the path of moral relativism, one
need not give up any of one's moral convictions, but must immediately relinquish any pretense that one holds these convictions for good reason.

Here, we will assume that there are objective grounds for
adhering to certain moral principles even if we cannot fully elaborate the basis for every belief in every case. The realist need
not be a moral Puritan nor need she believe that she always
knows what the right answer to every moral question is. Strong

reasons can be given, in realist fashion, for permitting great personal liberty in a variety of human contexts. Still, other reasons can be adduced for permitting personal choice where we are not certain what the proper answer to a moral question is. In short, one can be a moral realist and still believe that there are grounds for disagreement in some cases. Just as there is an answer to the scientific question of how the universe began, for example, while scientists may disagree about what that answer is, so too, lack of moral consensus does not entail that there is no right answer— that is, moral disagreement does not require moral relativism.

The Three Traditions of Moral Philosophy

If moral statements are indeed objectively true, what makes them so? Why is it that murder is wrong, exactly? What makes anything right or wrong in the first place? These questions have troubled moral philosophers for well over two millennia. Most generally, there exist three major traditions in Western philosophy that seek to answer the question: What makes one action or course of action better than another? The oldest of these three traditions, and one that is least in vogue today among moral philosophers, dates back to the fourth century B.C. and the time of Aristotle. Aristotle's system, which has been called "virtue ethics," elaborates the way in which an individual may become both happy and virtuous. (For Aristotle, happiness and virtue were not antithetical to one another as is commonly believed today. Quite the contrary, for Aristotle, virtue and happiness are each necessary for the other.) As such, Aristotle's theory is as much a *psychological* and *practical* theory as it is philosophical and theoretical. Aristotle's general theory will be described at some length in the following section. What is important to understand at this point is that his theory is very different from the two other realist theories yet to be described not only in that it is much older than these other two theories, but also because it is the only theory that has as its focus the actor, and not the action, as the basic unit of moral analysis.

Aristotle's theory looks to the development of the moral personality and to the inculcation of character. For Aristotle, "good" and "bad" are attributes applied to people, not actions per se. An act is good to the extent that it is the product of the virtuous character and the virtuous character is the hallmark of the good person. What is most important from a moral standpoint, however, is the genesis of any particular action, that is, that the act springs from virtuous character.

The other two objectivist moral traditions, generally known today as utilitarianism and deontology, have a number of interesting similarities. First, both were developed at about the same time at the end of the eighteenth century (though both also have roots in classical antiquity and the Christian era). Second, as mentioned previously, both theories focus upon the act as the basic quantum of moral analysis rather than on the actor. The "good person" is one who does good acts rather than the reverse. What utilitarianism and deontology do not share in common is their analysis of what makes a particular act good or bad, right or wrong.

Utilitarianism and deontology analyze the goodness or rightness of an action in two very different ways. The old moral query: "Does the end justify the means?" serves roughly to distinguish the two approaches. Modern utilitarianism, whose first systematic modern advocates were the English philosophers Jeremy Bentham and John Stuart Mill, believed that the moral measure of an action must be made in terms of its *consequences*. The best action is the one that promotes the best consequences or serves the most utility (thus the name, "utilitarianism"). Thus, properly qualified, the utilitarian would give an affirmative answer to the means-and-ends question mentioned above: if the good that is achieved in the end outweighs the bad that results in the means to that end—if, in short, there is a positive balance of good that results from the act—then the end will justify the means and the act will be considered good by the utilitarian.

The second tradition, deontology, holds that the rightness or wrongness of an action cannot be fully explained by an appeal to the consequences of an act. For the deontologist, certain acts are intrinsically right or wrong, independent of what consequences they may produce. Consider the following example: Suppose a jury deliberating at a trial could predict that a "not guilty" verdict would result in widespread riots, the deaths of dozens of innocent people, injuries to hundreds of others, and property damage in the hundreds of millions of dollars. By finding the defendants guilty, the jury could avert all this. If the jury were strict utilitarians, they might weigh the tumultuous consequences that would follow a "not guilty" verdict against the relatively minor (but also bad) consequences of finding innocent defendants guilty. As utilitarians, they might decide to find the defendants guilty and avert the disaster. The deontologist, on the other hand, would argue that cases such as this demonstrate that some acts (e.g., finding an innocent person guilty) are wrong even though they might produce the best consequences on balance.

Though modern deontology has its roots in the older religious traditions and, to a certain extent, in the natural law tradition, the eighteenth-century German philosopher Immanuel Kant is usually credited with being the first systematic exponent of the deontological view. There are a variety of strains of deontology, distinct in essential details from Kant's view, but all share the notion that there exist certain duties and rights that transcend the utilitarian weighing of consequences. The deontologist argues that she takes the individual more seriously than the utilitarian who, the deontologist argues, is willing to trade the rights of a few for the greater happiness of the many. Modern notions of equality, individual autonomy, and antimajoritarian rights have their philosophical roots in deontological thought.

Another way of viewing the distinction between the utilitarian approach and the deontological approach is that the utilitarian approach is said to be "forward looking," in that the utilitarian looks ahead to the consequences of his actions to determine their moral value, while the deontological approach is "backward looking." The deontologist asks whether an act is right or wrong in itself before considering the consequences. For the deontologist, the motive for performing an action is morally relevant to the moral value of the action, while, for the utilitarian, what matters are the consequences only.

For example, imagine that a small child who is about to drown in a pond is saved by someone passing by. Suppose the passerby saved the child because he realized that the child was from a very wealthy family and that he would be amply rewarded for the rescue. Suppose further that hope for reward is what *moti-*

vated the rescue such that he would not have come to the aid of a child if that child had been from a poorer family. The utilitarian is more likely to say that the rescue has the same moral value (the same goodness or rightness) whatever the motivation because the outcome, the consequence, is the same, that is, the child is saved. On the other hand, while the deontologist will be happy the child has been saved, he will nevertheless give the act a lower moral value because it has been done for a less-satisfying reason morally: actions motivated by hope of personal gain are of a lower moral value than those motivated by more altruistic intentions. Thus, the deontologist looks "backwards" to motives for actions, as well as to the nature of the acts themselves.

The three traditions of Western moral philosophy have influenced our law, our social institutions, and one another. Our moral thinking is often a patchwork quilt of these three approaches. Though there is probably no systematic way of reconciling these theories to one another, we often combine them in ad hoc and piecemeal fashion in our everyday moral thinking. Even the Constitution of the United States can be seen as a compromise or, more properly speaking, a *modus vivendi* between rule by the majority, which could be defended on utilitarian terms, and the protection of certain inalienable individual rights, a product of deontological and natural law thought.

In the following three sections, we will examine in greater detail virtue ethics, utilitarianism, and deontological thought. We will discuss the advantages as well as some of the classic objections to each respective theory.

Virtue Ethics: What Does It Mean to Be a Good Person?

In the *Ethica Nichomachea*, Aristotle put forth a theory of morality that has three main components: a metaphysical component, a psychological component, and an educational component. The metaphysical component provides that everything in the world has some essential purpose, function, or goal and that the "good" for any such object, living creature, or person is achieved when its innate purpose is most fully realized. This natural purpose or end, for which all things exist and into which all things strive to grow, is called that thing's *telos* (from which we get the word "teleology"). Each type of thing in the world has a different *telos*. The *telos* of the acorn is to become a full-grown oak tree; the *telos* of any utensil is to serve its purpose well (e.g., the *telos* of a chair is to provide a comfortable seating place for its occupant, etc.). The *telos* of any particular thing in the world serves as both a *description* of what goal or end that thing naturally aims at, and as a *prescription* insofar as the *telos* represents the goal at which we should aim in constructing an item or, indeed, in constructing ourselves to achieve our *telos* as human beings.

According to Aristotle, the *telos* or highest end toward which human beings strive is a state of contemplative happiness known as *eudamonia*. Eudamonia comes only when the individual has secured for himself or herself a position of social and economic security but also requires the development of virtue. "Virtue" here is not used in its Victorian sense to connote a restrained or repressed disposition to the good life and to worldly pleasures. Rather, virtue represents the golden mean between respective extreme alternative courses of action. The virtuous soldier is neither a coward nor is he brash; instead, he is courageous. The virtuous person in relation to others is neither a miser nor a profligate, but is generous. In life generally, virtue consists neither in ascetic self-denial nor in hedonistic self-indulgence. Rather, moderation is the way to happiness. In all matters, virtue represents the middle path between the extremes.

How, according to Aristotle, does one attain virtue? This brings us to the second, psychological component of his theory. Aristotle maintained that virtue is a self-perpetuating state of character that results from habitually doing what is right. (Vice, he notes, is similarly self-perpetuating.) The development of the virtuous character depends upon developing the capacity for "practical wisdom," a learned propensity for intuitively knowing what is right and for determining the best means to that end. Aristotle argues that "it is not possible to be wise in the strict sense without practical wisdom, nor practically wise without moral virtue." Both capacities develop together and each reinforces the other.

Finally, the third aspect of Aristotle's theory addresses the educational question: How can virtue be taught? Aristotle answers that virtue can only be gained if two things are done. First, the student must develop the capacity for practical wisdom and, second, virtue is dependent upon inculcation of good habits. By practical wisdom one gains an intuitive sense for what the right thing to do is and by the development of good habits one overcomes the psychological inertia that hinders the performance of such acts, even when we know what the right thing to do is.

In sum, Aristotle's moral theory seeks to show persons how to be good citizens and happy individuals. Happiness is dependent upon the development of virtue and virtue upon the development of both practical wisdom and good habits. With virtue, one habitually does what is right, where "doing what is right" fulfills our *telos* and leads to *eudamonia*, the highest form of happiness and the greatest realization of who we are essentially as human beings. In this way, our most fundamental moral aspirations are intimately tied up with our pursuit of existential fulfillment and psychological self-realization.

However, while Aristotle's theory tells us that happiness is achieved through virtue, and that virtue is the habitual performance of good deeds, how do we know what a good deed is in the first place? What would Aristotle's theory say of the moral permissibility of abortion, premarital sex, the justness of capital punishment, or any of a range of other social and moral issues? Indeed, Aristotle seems to *assume* which practices are permissible and which are not. At some points, the modern mind is in accordance with his assumptions; Aristotle counseled generosity to the poor, for example. At other points, however, we find his moral conclusions abominable: he advocated slavery for the barbarian and the political subjugation of women.

Perhaps because Aristotle lived in a relatively closed community and at a morally conservative time, in great contrast to the modern tendency to question virtually every practice, he did not challenge some of the moral assumptions which were then persuasive. This was left largely to the modern mind and to a refocusing of moral analysis from the actor and onto the action itself.

Nonetheless, Aristotle's ethical theory is the most practical of the three that we will discuss here, at least to the individual, insofar as it prescribes a method for attaining virtue and happiness. In one section of chapter 3, we will discuss the relationship between virtue ethics, optimum mental health, and vegetarianism.

Utilitarianism: The Problem with Happiness

Fully twenty centuries after Aristotle, modern utilitarianism was born. It was late eighteenth-century Europe. The Age of Reason was in full flower and the spirit of reform was thick in the air. It was the time of the American and French revolutions, of the spread of scientific ideas and recent medical discoveries. It was the period of some of the greatest minds of Western civilization: Voltaire, Diderot, Rousseau, Hume, Kant, Thomas Reid, Adam Smith, Jefferson, and Franklin to name but a few. It was a time of incredible intellectual and artistic achievement. And it was in this exhilarating intellectual and social milieu that utilitarianism's first exponent, the English philosopher and lawyer Jeremy Bentham lived.

Bentham's life goal was to abolish the static and repressive religious morality that had reigned for centuries, replacing it with a system of morality predicated upon reason and humanity. Morality, he asserted, must not be based on otherworldly dogma, "immutable" natural law principles, or the pronouncements of a deity whose very existence was increasingly questioned, but should be predicated instead on the very worldly notion that the ultimate goal of morality is to promote human happiness. His life's work was to reform both the civil and criminal law of England, which continued to prescribe the death penalty for over two hundred offenses including petty theft and adultery, and to transform the prevailing notions of morality, which underwrote the law.

The philosophical vehicle for achieving these utilitarian aims was Bentham's Greatest Happiness Principle. The Greatest Happiness Principle requires that, in evaluating a law or a moral rule or, for that matter, any individual course of conduct, the consequences of adopting that rule or course of conduct be compared to the consequences of every alternative rule or course of conduct. Whichever act or rule produces the greatest happiness (or most reduces the painful consequences) for the greatest number of persons is the one that should be adopted. Utilitarians called this mathematical weighing of advantages and disadvantages, cast in terms of the overall pleasure to be achieved, the "hedonic calculus" (as in the term "hedonism").

The hedonic calculus was immediately employed in evaluating a variety of social taboos and legal proscriptions. An example will demonstrate how the calculus works: in deciding whether prostitution should be decriminalized, the hedonic calculus requires that we calculate the net utility in legalized prostitution versus the net utility in continuing to criminalize it. This would involve calculating all the happiness to be gained by permitting prostitution (e.g., to prostitutes, their customers) along with any secondary social benefits and disadvantages subtracting from this whatever negative utility results from such a scheme (e.g., from increased venereal disease or other social ills associated with prostitution), and comparing this total sum to the total obtained in making a similar calculation for the rule prohibiting prostitution. If more happiness is achievable by legalization, then centuries of religious and moral disapprobation should be cast aside in favor of permitting prostitution. That prostitution should be legalized is exactly the conclusion reached in 1957 by England's Wolfenden Commission, members of which were undoubtedly influenced by the tenets of utilitarianism and the Greatest Happiness Principle.

Obviously, the calculations can often become quite complicated, particularly in looking at proposals that would affect large segments of the population and where some of the consequences are speculative. For example, how many people will avail themselves of the legal prostitute who are currently prevented from doing so by the law? And how much happiness will be gained?

Further, will the advantages and disadvantages, and their quantitative values change as a result of implementing one course of action rather than another? For example, many argue that, were prostitution to become legal, the government could regulate the spread of venereal diseases; also, the negative social stigma associated with sex-for-money exchanges might be eliminated as prostitution became socially acceptable. On the other hand, would sex itself become devalued as a result of legalized prostitution such that the gains from legalization diminish with time?

Thus, the long-term consequences of any scheme might alter the outcome of the calculations and must be factored into the equation. Bentham and other utilitarians, including John Stuart Mill, would have admitted that the hedonic calculus might be very complicated. They would have welcomed this charge, however, as a natural consequence of the utilitarian system, which sought to be as scientific and quantitative as possible.

In its origin and operation, utilitarianism is in a sense the most social of the three traditions of realist moral philosophy. It was initially developed as a theory to reform the law and, because of its emphasis on interpersonal calculations of happiness, it lends itself more readily to deciding questions of legislation than does either virtue ethics or deontology. (Imagine trying to vote on a farm subsidy bill or whether to raise taxes on the basis of virtue ethics or deontology.) As we shall see, however, it is precisely the interpersonal dimension of utilitarianism that has led to an important objection raised by critics.

The question of what the utilitarian means by "happiness," exactly, has also been a matter of controversy. Bentham equated happiness with pleasure and unhappiness with pain. This has led to a series of conundrums and contradictions: for example, the masochist who appears to derive happiness from pain. It has also led to the objection that utilitarianism is an ignoble moral theory that fosters a lowly view of human nature. If goodness is equated with pleasure, the critics ask, then are all "lower" pleasures, however tawdry and venal, carnal or base, to be equated with other "higher" pleasures? Is the pleasure obtained in the course of debauchery to be sanctioned in equal measure with that gained from intellectual achievement? Is it better on utilitarian theory, as it is sometimes said, to be a happy idiot rather than a sad Socrates?

The impact of utilitarianism both in moral theory and in the development of Anglo-American law has been very significant. Moreover, the utilitarian's quest to convert subjective choices into quantitatively precise descriptions of behavior has influenced other disciplines as well, including nineteenth- and twentieth-century economic theory, game theory, and certain psychological models of human interaction. Nevertheless, though utilitarianism may be useful in making certain kinds of decisions, there are also a number of fundamental limitations with utilitarianism as a comprehensive moral system. Most basically, criticisms have focused on three general problems, what we might call the problems of quantification, of happiness, and of justice.

The most practical of the three problems is the problem of quantification. The problem, most basically, is that the quest to determine the relative amounts of pleasure and pain in a given plan or course of action is illusory. First, how can one person's pleasure be quantified against another person's pleasure such that it is possible to say which quantity is higher? Indeed, as the critic points out, it is often difficult for individuals to compare two competing pleasures even within the limited context of their own individual preferences. To take a prosaic example, a person's attempt to determine whether she will receive more pleasure from going to a ball game or a play on a given spare evening may be difficult enough. Not only does the hedonic calculus require this prioritization, it also requires that exact quantities must be assigned for alternative choices such that the ball game is worth x units of happiness and the play y units.

This same problem goes from difficult to intractable when the necessary weighing and assignment of points must be made between two or more persons and when the types of pleasure and pain to be expected and compared are very different. In the case of the legalization of prostitution, how does one weigh the net "gain" in sexual satisfaction to be experienced by one segment of the population against the disadvantages inherent in legalizing prostitution, for example, the displeasure of those who must countenance such activity in their neighborhoods? To take another example, how is one to weigh the environmental damage caused by permitting commercial logging against the lost jobs and economic harms inherent in preventing it? It requires the impossible weighing of apples and oranges, this criticism maintains. Add to this the problem of calculating speculative or uncertain consequences—for example, whether legalizing prostitution will increase or decrease criminal sexual assaults—and the problem of calculating the significance of relatively more abstract consequences—for example, will legalizing prostitution lead to a dehumanized view of women?—and the problem of quantification appears to be insurmountable.

The general response by the utilitarian is to freely admit the problem but to say that we must do the best we can with the information we have. If there are problems inherent in quantifying the consequences of certain actions, they might add, how much more vague and ambiguous must be other forms of moral reasoning that do not consider these consequences at all? The utilitarian's response here is plausible. Minimally, however, he must admit that the goal for mathematical certainty is exactly that—simply a goal. To achieve this kind of certainty in reality is pure illusion.

The second objection to utilitarianism, the problem of happiness, is more theoretical. This objection holds that happiness or pleasure cannot constitute the be-all and end-all of moral analysis. There must be other moral considerations than the hedonistic aspect of actions. For example, is murder really wrong, as the utilitarian seems to imply, because the murderer is depriving his victim of a life of pleasure? What, for example, if we could say with certainty that a particular victim was going to experience more pain than pleasure, on balance, for the rest of her life? Our intuitions tell us that murder would still be wrong even though, on a strictly utilitarian account, the murderer appears to be doing the victim a favor.

The objection has been cast in more imaginative terms as well. Suppose a scientist were to create a machine called an "orgasmatron." By hooking up to the machine, any person could guarantee that he experience the pure, unadulterated pleasure of an orgasm continuously for months, years, even the rest of his life. The pleasure would far surpass in quantity the pleasure one might expect to experience in the course of a normal life. Yet, our intuitions tell us again that this would be a life wasted, that there are more important things to do with one's life than lie back and passively experience pleasure for the rest of one's days.

The problem of happiness points to a basic limitation in the moral analysis of utilitarianism. There are other values such as love, freedom, intellectual or artistic excellence, self-sufficiency, or development of moral character, which, while they may bring a modicum of pleasure, are not wholly reducible to the pleasure

or happiness they bring. Indeed, at times we see fit to make great
sacrifices for these other values, all of which seems to indicate
that we are not moved by pleasure alone.

It should be noted that some modern utilitarians have accepted such charges and have changed the focus of utilitarianism from
the pursuit of happiness, narrowly defined, to the quest for these
other values. "Preference utilitarians" look to the maximization
of human choices, rather than pleasure, while "pluralistic utilitarians" believe that no one value such as pleasure will suffice
to explain and justify our moral intuitions; many values, including those mentioned above, count in the moral calculation. While
the problem of happiness is partially met by these refinements,
there are still other problems inherent in these newer forms of
utilitarianism.

It is the third type of objection to utilitarianism, however,
which cuts the deepest and serves to demonstrate the most profound of the inherent shortcomings of classical utilitarian theory; this is the problem of justice. Imagine the following scenario:
Social scientists of a particularly virulent utilitarian bent conclude, on the basis of research and calculation, that the net utility (the overall level of pleasure) for the entire society could be
dramatically increased if we made one important change in social structure. We would enslave 20 percent of the population,
who would be forced to do the hardest work, the most menial
and unsatisfying jobs, so that the remaining 80 percent could live
well. While this 20 percent would, of course, experience a net
decline in their level of happiness, this would be more than offset by the gain in net utility for the other 80 percent. Utilitarian
theory seems to require just such a move if, in fact, the net increase in happiness could be achieved in this manner. (Note that
the scenario mentioned earlier, in which innocent defendants are
convicted to prevent a riot, is another version of this same objection.) The problem for utilitarian theory is that it seems to
permit—even to require—that certain individuals be sacrificed for
the greater happiness of the whole.

The problem of justice has been variously described as the
problem of not taking the differences between individuals seriously, or of not observing that there exist certain rights that serve
as "trumps" or limits on the extent to which one person's happi-

ness may be sacrificed for another's. It is a problem of justice insofar as every individual is due certain rights and privileges that cannot be traded off, either by her or by others on her behalf.

The utilitarian case for vegetarianism will proceed on five distinct bases: that utilitarian principles are violated by (1) the current, prevailing practices of livestock production (chapter 2), (2) the needless slaughter of animals (chapter 2), (3) the ill effects of meat eating upon human health and well-being (chapter 3), (4) the disastrous effects of meat production upon the environment, which have indirect effects upon humans everywhere (chapter 4), and (5) the relationship between meat production and world hunger (chapter 5). Note that the first two bases focus on animal suffering, while the latter three emphasize the effects of meat consumption upon humans.

Deontological Thought: Rights, Interests, and the Question as to Who Counts

Classical deontology, as formulated by the German philosopher, Immanuel Kant stands virtually at as great a logical distance from the principles of utilitarianism as any theory possibly could. Kant's theory was laid out in a small book entitled *Grounding for the Metaphysics of Morals*, published in 1785, just four years before Jeremy Bentham's *Introduction to the Principles of Morals and Legislation*. Kant's work is a masterpiece of moral insight and philosophy and, even today, inspires the reader with the sense of noble purpose and conviction with which it was undeniably written.

Kant's approach was radically distinct from that of the utilitarians. His quest, he stated, was to find the "supreme principle of morality." His view ultimately rejects as the basis for what makes an act good or bad the satisfaction of human desires, emotions, hopes, pleasures, and other sentiments. While the moral world of the utilitarian is a world of costs and benefits played out in terms of the net amount of pleasure gained by a particular act, Kant's moral world is dominated by the concept of duty. Indeed, the term "deontology," later used to describe Kant's theory, comes from the Greek word *deon*, meaning "duty."

According to Kant's theory, the good act is the act performed not for some end, purpose, or consequence—whether this be the satisfaction of some desire or the attainment of the greatest happiness for the greatest number—but is the act that is performed in accordance with certain principles established by reason.

What might these principles be? Kant begins by asking: What is intrinsically good, that is, good in and of itself? He goes through a list of possibilities, such as wealth, intelligence, health, physical strength or attractiveness, and concludes that none of these are intrinsically good since each can be put toward some evil end. The only thing good in and of itself, it turns out, is "the good will." What is the "good will," you now ask. It is the will that acts, first, *in accordance with* duty and, second, *for the sake of* duty. In other words, to be a morally good act, a person must not only perform the right act (i.e., the act that is in accordance with duty), but also must perform it with the right intention (i.e., for the sake of duty). And it is reason that tells us what our duty is, exactly.

Reason also has a second function in Kant's moral theory. It is only in the exercise of what Kant calls "the practical reason" that we are, properly speaking, moral creatures at all. It is our capacity to reason that makes us worthy of the moral recognition of others. Indeed, Kant held reason in such high esteem that he suggested that even the performance of a good act out of some altruistic emotion such as sympathy was morally inferior to an act similarly performed out of the motive to act simply according to duty and as reason requires.

Reason is also instrumental in Kant's emphasis on individual responsibility. Kant lived at the time of the rebirth of science. His century witnessed as science began to explain all natural phenomena in terms of scientific laws. These natural laws explained the movement of the planets around the sun, the seasons, the growth and behavior of plants and animals, and all other natural occurrences. But is not humankind also a part of nature? And, as such, are we not equally subject to these causal laws? If human behavior, as a part of nature, is a product of the same natural laws that govern everything else in nature, then how can a human being be any more responsible for his or her behavior, in an ultimate sense, than the planets are responsible for their revolution around the sun?

Kant accepted the scientific account of natural phenomena but argued that in the exercise of reason, in particular, the practical reason, human beings alone can escape this web of causal necessity. The practical reason was, for Kant, a combination of reason and free will; it represents the capacity we have as human beings to resist temptation and to do what is right—that is, to act in accordance with duty and for the sake of duty—even when doing so is not in our own self-interest. It is only in the exercise of practical reason that we are moral beings at all.

Reason recognizes that the only thing that is good in an unqualified sense is the good will, and that the good will requires that we act in accordance with duty and for the sake of duty. But what exactly is our duty?

The substance of our duties is contained in what Kant calls the "categorical imperative." Kant actually elaborates two versions of the categorical imperative, which he appears to have thought were logically equivalent principles. The first version of the categorical imperative provides that we must never use another moral being (i.e., anyone capable of reason and free will) as a means to our own ends. Instead, we must always treat every person as an end in herself. The second version of the categorical imperative holds that we must always act in a manner such that we could wish that every person similarly situated would act in the same way.

Kant argued that his categorical imperative was binding on all in the moral community and protected all in the moral community. Moreover, all members of the moral community must be treated equally because they are, in their most essential aspect as persons, equal as moral beings. Moral equality does not require intellectual, social, or economic equality. Rather, it merely requires the potential to be capable of reasoning and the exercise of free will. From Kant's moral theory, modern liberal political theory has inherited its emphasis on equality, its attention to the moral worth of every individual, and its reverence for personal autonomy.

What has been said by way of criticizing Kant's theory? Philosophers have argued for two centuries now over a number of theoretical and interpretational problems including Kant's dubious claim that a violation of the categorical imperative constitutes a logical contradiction on the part of the actor. We need not address these problems here. Rather, we must note two more significant difficulties for our purposes and for the purposes of applied philosophy generally. The first problem is with Kant's notion of moral community. To be a member of the moral community—that is, to be bound by duties and the subject of rights—one must be capable of the exercise of practical reason. Roughly speaking, one must be able to reason in a self-conscious manner and must be able to exercise his or her free will. Kant does not deny that we have certain other duties to those outside of the moral community, but the categorical imperative does not apply to actions not involving a member of the moral community.

This position appears to leave many, perhaps most, animals out of the moral community. To put it differently, there are no "animal rights" in Kantian theory. Kant's conclusion in this respect is as much the result of a psychological assumption about the mental life of animals as it is a moral premise. Because of its importance to the case for vegetarianism, we will return to this problem at greater length in chapter 2.

The second problem with Kant's moral theory is that, in one important sense, it really does not tell us much at all. Put differently, it is difficult to see how the theory should be applied to a variety of real-world moral problems. Unlike utilitarianism, Kantian deontology goes little way in telling us how to decide certain macro-moral problems that typically face legislators. For example, utilizing Kantian deontology, how even in theory can we resolve the dispute between commercial interests and environmentalists in deciding whether to prohibit commercial logging? At least utilitarianism gives us a framework for weighing the interests at stake. Similarly, what does deontology tell us about the abortion debate? Kant himself would have been opposed to abortion except perhaps in the case of saving a woman's life. Yet, today the pro-choice movement is cast in terms of a *right* to self-determination on the part of a woman, a type of deontological defense of abortion.

What happens in situations where conflicts in duties arise? For example, we have a duty, Kant says, never to lie. We also have a duty to keep our promises. To use a somewhat overworked but still highly effective example, what should we do when we promise to protect a Jewish family and Nazi soldiers show up at our door inquiring as to whether we have seen any stray Jews in the area? Do we lie or do we break our promise? There are an infinite number of other, more prosaic examples of such conflicts. Again, at least utilitarianism gives us a way of comparing these competing concerns.

With its emphasis on individual duties, Kantian theory shares with virtue ethics both an inspired moral view of human nature and an inherent inability to tell us how to apply the theory in real situations. The Kantian might respond to all this by saying simply that, beyond the two versions of the categorical imperative, there are no formulae but that formulae are not necessary. What is important is that people separate out their own interest in an outcome when engaging in moral deliberation. What we must learn to do, the Kantian might say, is to dissociate ourselves from our moral deliberations such that we do not give our personal interest any greater weight than that of any other moral being. Then, we must always act in ways that we would have others act if placed in our situation. This, at least, would take us much closer to the spirit of deontological thought.

It should be noted in closing that there are a variety of modern versions of deontological moral theory, some of which we will discuss in the next chapter. Some of these, such as the intuitionism of W. D. Ross, are modern attempts to refine deontological thought, answering criticisms raised against Kantianism. Other theories represent a plethora of very different political and social views, ranging from the traditionally liberal to the radically conservative, which have sprung from deontological roots. These include various forms of libertarianism, modern contractarianism, and social rights theories propounded by defenders of the welfare state. What all of these share in common is their emphasis on rights and duties as the ultimate moral categories, a far cry indeed from the Greatest Happiness Principle of the utilitarians.

Arguments versus Intuitions

Having surveyed the three traditions of Western moral thought along with their attendant problems and shortcomings, the question might now arise: Why does any of this matter, anyway? If none of these various theories can do the job of justifying certain heartfelt moral conclusions, then so much the worse for these theories. If we know something is wrong intuitively and our moral theory cannot explain why, then something must be wrong with that theory, not with our intuitions. If no theory can explain moral goodness or badness, rightness or wrongness, then maybe something is wrong with moral argument and theory generally. Perhaps moral intuitions simply cannot be explained, in that case, why bother with arguments?

This type of impasse often occurs in moral debates. Some time ago I became involved in a discussion with another vegetarian on the subject of animal rights. At one point, she asserted that animals have as much of a "right to life" as do people. (This is an issue that will be taken up in chapter 2.) I asked her what reason she had for believing this, to which she responded, "Why does there always have to be a reason? Why can't you just go by your intuitions?" Why do we need arguments at all? Why not go on feeling?

While it is natural even for a philosopher in his better moments to feel a certain sympathy for this position—let's call it "pragmatic intuitionism"—the problem with this approach is straightforward enough: some people's feelings and intuitions often differ from those of other people. When one person has the intuition that meat eating is morally abominable and another has the intuition that it is perfectly justified, who is right? Both may feel their feelings equally strongly and with an equal sense of moral indignation. When this occurs, how do we decide who is right?

One reply to this is to say that neither is right and neither is wrong—they are just different moral intuitions. But this reply throws the baby out with the bathwater. It is a return to moral relativism. If neither person is right, then vegetarianism is not morally preferable to meat eating—indeed, there are no objective moral preferences at all—and the vegetarian has no business trying to convince the steak eater that it is. If, on the other hand, vegetarianism is morally preferable, then there must be something that *makes it so.*

We could, of course, simply take a vote. Whichever side musters the most votes would carry the day. Of course, this approach does not bode well for the vegetarian, who is in a distinct minority. Nor is vote counting a reliable way of settling vexing moral questions. To paraphrase Voltaire, the majority is often wrong. Further, although an appeal to majority vote may sound like a democratic way to settle a moral issue, it has strange implications for our concept of morality. As the vote on any moral issue changed, so too would its moral status. For example, slavery would have been morally permissible in the South of the 1850s, when the majority thought it permissible, but impermissible in the South today. The rightness or wrongness of things would vary from place to place and even from time to time in a particular place. We would be back to cultural relativism with all its difficulties.

Finally, we could say that the intuitions of certain people are more "evolved" or developed than the intuitions of others. So, the reasoning runs, we ought to listen to the more evolved in their rendition of what is morally required. But who is to say who has more "evolved" intuitions? Some standard is necessary to judge respective levels of moral evolution and then we are back to our quest for some objective basis for morality. We could, of course, assert that the level of moral evolution can be determined from the conclusions one draws. In other words, the better the moral conclusions one draws, the more evolved that person is. However, this response is blatantly circular: We want to know whether one person's intuition is better than another's so we seek to determine this by their level of "evolution." How do we determine a person's level of evolution? By the conclusions he or she draws. Round and round we go in never-ending fashion.

If feelings or intuitions alone will not suffice as the arbiter of moral disputes, are these feelings and intuitions completely useless, excess emotional baggage to be cast aside as soon as a logical argument is within sight? Some philosophers have adopted this extreme position, but these thinkers are in the minority. A more popular and recent position has been that we must seek to achieve a fit between our feelings and intuitions, on one hand, and the conclusions our arguments lead us to, on the other hand. The philosopher John Rawls calls the result of this process "reflective equilibrium."

The process of reflective equilibrium works in the following fashion: We begin with an intuition such as "murder is wrong." We seek to justify that feeling by appealing to moral theory or argument. If the theory does not succeed in justifying that feeling, the theory may be wrong. In some cases, however, our feelings may be wrong, or inconsistent with still other moral feelings. Argument fulfills the function of systematizing our feelings and beliefs. It forces us to be consistent. If we believe, for example, that killing is wrong and explain this feeling by appealing to moral theory, saying for example that killing is wrong because it is wrong to deprive any sentient creature of life, we have found a justification for our feeling that killing is wrong.

But what if we also happen to eat meat regularly? We are then confronted with a three-way choice: first, we might rationalize our behavior by concluding that animals are not sentient creatures, a dubious proposition. Second, we might change our explanation as to why killing is wrong, finding a theory that leaves in humans while leaving out animals. We might appeal to a theory that says, for example, that it is only wrong to kill beings who stand on two legs, or that it is only wrong to kill beings who can do college algebra. (Note that these theories have problems of their own. First, of course, they are implausible: a theory must not only justify our moral intuitions, it must *explain* them; in other words, it must explain why we feel that a particular act is wrong. Insofar as we seem to feel that murder would still be wrong even if humans had four legs, for example, we can see that this reason is inadequate. Second, the theories may be overinclusive and underinclusive in their scope. Chickens would still be covered by a theory that held that murder is wrong because it is the killing of a two-legged creature, and all too many humans would be excluded by the second criteria, the ability to do college algebra.)

As a third alternative, we might accept that vegetarianism is entailed by our own moral theory. In this case, of course, to be consistent we should conform our behavior to the moral conclusion we have drawn and relinquish the habit of meat eating. Whichever of the three choices we adopt, however, will be the result of attempting to find a fit between our moral intuitions, our theoretical justification for these intuitions and certain other empirical or factual propositions necessary to the moral argument (e.g., whether animals are sentient or conscious creatures).

Of course, there is a fourth possibility as well—a possibility that is, unfortunately, both the most popular and the least rational alternative. We can simply ignore the contradiction between our theoretical justification and our behavior. This is a nonresponse, even if an all-too-frequent one.

The Importance of Applied Moral Thought and the Case for Vegetarianism

In the following chapters, the case for vegetarianism will be divided up, chapter by chapter, by major issues or types of concern (e.g., animal rights, health, the environment), rather than by types of philosophical theory. Within each chapter a mix of moral theories, generally utilitarianism and deontology, will provide the basis for each argument. In some cases, the type of issue will lend itself best to analysis on utilitarian terms. For example, the argument from health is best cast in terms of the net benefits to be achieved by the individual and society at large by adopting a vegetarian diet. Other arguments are primarily deontological in character—for example, the case for animal rights. At other points, there will be a mix of these arguments. For example, there is also a utilitarian argument for the protection of animals. Indeed, some of the conclusions will be justified on alternative theories. Thus, the argument from world hunger can be played out either in terms of the rights of those affected by famine or in terms of the benefits to everyone by preventing world hunger.

It is important to note that, except for portions of chapter 2, the theory as we have described it will remain in the background, illuminating our discussion but not dominating it. At points, the relevance of many of the issues discussed in this first chapter will become clear, as will the reason for elaborating some of the objections to some of these various theories. Generally, however, the discussion will be less theoretical and considerably more factual and applied as compared with the present chapter. This is only fitting in a book that seeks, as this does, to use philosophy as a means for solving a real-world moral question. In essence, moral theory will remain a backdrop, a departure point, from which we will launch an applied moral investigation of the argument for vegetarianism.

Finally, a word is in order concerning the way we will use moral theory—or more properly, *which* moral theory we will use to establish our conclusions. It is my belief that the case for vegetarianism can be made on either utilitarian or deontological grounds. More generally, however, the philosophical theory to be employed here—and the analysis I believe to come closest to explaining and justifying my most heartfelt moral intuitions generally—will be a two-tier system. The first-level analysis is deontological. We must ask first whether a particular practice (e.g., meat eating) violates the rights of another affected class (in this case, animals). If it does, we need go no further. A utilitarian justification for meat eating cannot override a deontological proscription of it. In other words, if animals can be ascribed genuine rights, the fact that there may be a utilitarian advantage to us as humans in eating meat can no more justify our doing so than did the advantage of averting riots justify a false guilty verdict in our earlier example. If, on the other hand, there are no violations of rights, then we can proceed with the second utilitarian level of the analysis.

The book is constructed with this framework in mind. It is my contention in chapter 2 that animals are aware of their own lives, though perhaps not in as self-conscious a manner as humans, and should be protected from unnecessary killing for that reason alone. Even if the reader does not join me in that conclusion, however, the book proceeds on largely utilitarian grounds (though, again, utilitarianism and deontology will be interspersed throughout).

As I close this chapter, I wish to end with a confession of sorts. Notwithstanding our reliance upon analysis and argument throughout this chapter and this book, and though I believe wholeheartedly in the process of rational justification for our moral beliefs, the argument for vegetarianism does not begin with analysis or argument; it ends with these. *Analysis justifies and explains but intuition inspires and motivates.* Throughout the book, I will do what I can to make clear my underlying intuitions, both because they may not be shared by others and because of their sheer moral force in driving not only this book, but also my conversion thirteen years ago to vegetarianism.

Chapter Two

The Argument from the Rights and Interests of Animals

Before the American Civil War, perhaps the greatest ideological obstacle faced by the abolitionist movement was to demonstrate to the satisfaction of slaveholders and others that there was no *morally relevant* difference between whites and blacks. If it was beyond dispute, as a reasonable slaveowner would have admitted, that it would be wrong to enslave a person of European descent, then it was also wrong to enslave the African *unless* there was some difference between the two that was so compelling that it could justify such radically different treatment. Despite our modern incredulity, defenders of slavery argued that such radical differences did exist. And the fact that the propriety of slaveholding went virtually unquestioned by large segments of antebellum society is sufficient demonstration of the nearly overwhelming human capacity to overlook injustice, at least when we think it happens to benefit us in doing so.

A similar problem confronts the modern vegetarian or advocate of animal rights. If we accept, as surely most do, that it is wrong (under most circumstances) to kill humans, then it is also wrong to kill animals for food unless there is some *morally relevant* difference between humans and animals. Of course, many today accept that there are such differences just as many others accepted the differences between the races a century and a half ago.

Why is it, exactly, that murder is wrong—at least when it is the murder of a human being we are speaking of? And why should this reason by applicable to humans only? In answering these questions, we must be careful not to permit our precondi-

31

tioned cultural prejudices to influence our answers. We must think these problems out anew for ourselves.

In considering this problem here, we will begin by examining religious attitudes, particularly those of Christianity, as they relate to the treatment of animals. The first attempt to distinguish humans from animals, after all, holds that what makes us different from animals is our possession of an immortal soul.

Religious Ambiguity and the
Moral Status of Animals

All modern religions have injunctions against killing as one of their central tenets. From the proscription of Exodus that "thou shalt not kill" to the Buddhist doctrine of *ahimsa* or nonviolence, the rule is clear: killing is forbidden. What is less clear is the application of this rule. The scope of creatures to which the injunction extends varies not only from religion to religion, but also among different branches of each religion and sometimes within the same religion at different times in its history.

For example, original Buddhism was perhaps the most clear on the sacredness of all life. The doctrine of *ahimsa*, which is said to have originated with the teachings of the Buddha himself in the sixth century B.C., required nonviolence to all sentient creatures. Vegetarianism was a fundamental application of this principle. Today, however, a majority of Buddhists, those representing the Mahayana (or "greater raft," for its larger number of followers) tradition, predominant in China, Korea, Mongolia, and Japan, do not require vegetarianism. Hinayana ("lesser raft") Buddhism, with its greatest influence in Southeast Asia, Cambodia, Vietnam, and Thailand, observes a form of practice arguably much closer in teaching to that of original Buddhism. Vegetarianism is more widespread among the Hinayana Buddhists. Nevertheless, perhaps as a result of the schism, one story, undoubtedly propagated by Mahayana Buddhists, holds that the Buddha himself ate meat (an extremely unlikely proposition) and attributes his death to a meal of bad pork.

Similarly, Hinduism, today known for its strict adherence to vegetarianism and its devoted reverence to the cow, was, early in its history, a religion predicated upon animal sacrifice. Much of early Hindu culture was based upon cattle—cattle raiding, cattle sacrifice, and cattle as the chief source of property. Even the Vedic word for "war" was "desire for cattle." In the third and fourth centuries B.C., the Hindu Brahmin caste survived the popular uprisings that were brought about in part by their cattle hoarding only by incorporating Buddhist principles into their own religious practices. The cow was elevated to the status of a near-deity and vegetarianism prescribed for all. (Buddhism was also influential in the development of Jainism, a religion still practiced today by a few million people in India and Iran, which requires strict adherence to a vegetarian diet.) Thus, Eastern religions have often, though not universally, accorded animals a favorable status.

In the West, the religious attitude toward animals has been considerably more ambivalent and sometimes hostile. With the exception of a number of rules governing the way in which animals are to be killed, and which animals are to be eaten in the first place, modern adherents of Judaism and Islam have little in the way of religious doctrine concerning our treatment of animals. With few exceptions (e.g. rules prescribing the speedy slaughter of animals), even where rules exist, they have been motivated largely by concerns for human health rather than any particular sympathy for the animal itself. Similarly, with the exception of a few sects such as the Seventh Day Adventists, vegetarianism is not viewed as a requirement of most forms of modern Christianity.

Nevertheless, a strong case can be made for the claim that the first Christians observed a vegetarian diet. There is a good deal of textual support for the requirement of vegetarianism among Christians. For example, Exodus closes:

> For that which befalleth the
> Sons of men befalleth beasts,
> Even one thing befalleth them,
> As one dieth, so dieth the other;
> Yea, they have all one breath,
> So that a man hath no preeminence
> Above a beast, for all is vanity.

Similarly, from Genesis there is strong suggestion both that animals have souls and that vegetarianism is part of the faith.

> Here, God proclaims:
> And to every beast of the earth
> And to every foul of the air,
> And to everything that creepeth
> Upon the earth wherein there is a
> Living soul, I have given every
> Green herb for meat.

There is some evidence that all of the Apostles were vegetarian. Homily VII, attributed to the teaching of St. Peter, declares, "The unnatural eating of flesh-meats is as polluting as the heathen worship of devils; with its sacrifices and its impure feasts through participation in which a man becomes a fellow eater with devils."[1] Among early Christian theologians and church fathers, the following are claimed by one source to have been vegetarians: St. Jerome, Tertullian, St. John Crysosthum, St. Benedict, Clement, Pliny, Eusebius, Papias, Cyprian, and Pantaenus.[2] If this is true, it would certainly lend strong support to the argument that early Christians interpreted Christ's teachings to require a vegetarian diet.

But there is equally strong support against the view that vegetarianism was required. The Old Testament is peppered with accounts of animal sacrifice, often mandated by God. From the New Testament we have, among other stories, the account of Christ providing loaves and fish to the wedding party he happened across. In Corinthians, Paul also states that man may eat whatever he wishes, including meat. How are these to be reconciled with the claim that Christ himself advocated vegetarianism?

One explanation with some historical foundation holds that Christianity did require vegetarianism until roughly the fourth century A.D. In 325, the Council of Nicea was convened in order to reformulate Christianity to make it more palatable to the Roman emperor, Constantine. The story holds that the church fathers sold out some of the more easily abandoned aspects of Christian teaching, including vegetarianism, in exchange for the

Emperor's conversion and the political sanction that came with recognition as a state religion. After this time, not only was vegetarianism no longer required, it was deemed a heresy that was rewarded by death—and a particularly unpleasant death at that. It is reported that Constantine ordered that any Christian caught practicing vegetarianism should be punished by having molten lead poured down his throat.

Whether vegetarianism is required by Christian doctrine involves, of course, answering a nest of questions, theological and exegetical, historical and interpretational, for example whether it is "faith" or "works" that is most important to having one's soul saved. The theological question that dominates the debate, however, is the question as to whether animals possess souls. If, according to Christian doctrine, animals do have souls, there is good reason for believing that they should be treated just as people are; in other words, we should not feed on them. But through the influence of subsequent Christian philosophers, particularly St. Augustine and St. Thomas Aquinas, the notion that animals had souls was repudiated. (Indeed, Aquinas apparently believed that even women did not have souls, though he grudgingly accepted, as a public matter, the conclusion of the Church to the contrary.)

While some philosophers have argued that religious doctrine supports the conclusion that animals do have souls, an equally compelling argument can be made that vegetarianism is all the more obligatory if it turns out that animals do not possess souls: If animals *do* have souls, then the death of an animal's physical body will not mean the end of its existence; its soul will go on to live in the afterlife. In this case, eating animal bodies is not quite so morally objectionable. But if this same animal possesses no immortal soul, ending its physical life entails a far greater—indeed, an infinite—loss to it. Its entire existence is ended once and for all. Thus, vegetarianism may be required either way—whether or not animals possess an immortal soul.

With the rejection of the existence of souls, human or otherwise, that came with the eighteenth and nineteenth centuries and the Age of Reason, scientists and philosophers cast about in search of another way to distinguish animals from humans. Their

conclusions often had more shocking and brutal consequences for
animals than had the speculation of their Christian predecessors.

Stewardship, Dominion, or Exploitation: A Short History of Ideas on the Relationship between Humankind and the Animal Kingdom

Though the early Christian was no environmental progressive,
and while he or she would have scoffed at the notion of animal
rights, neither did he or she believe one had the right to do with
the natural world as one wished. Despite the various shortcomings of Christian theology from the standpoint of deep ecology
and animal rights, the Christian still had obligations—if not to
animals, then to God. The Christian viewed his or her obligations to the natural world, including the animal kingdom, as one
of stewardship. People were God's managers-in-residence on
earth. It was the obligation of people to protect and develop God's
Creation, preserving it both for the next generation—to the extent they thought there would be a next generation—and for
God's pleasure.

The concept of stewardship, so central to the Christian ethic,
held that people did not inherit the earth from the previous generation; they borrowed it, with God's permission, from the next.
As such, people had an obligation to preserve the natural bounty
of the land, to take only what they needed, to use it wisely and
to restore what they had taken.

The concept of stewardship, however, easily degenerated into
the superficially similar notion of dominion. If people were to
manage the earth with its reserves of game, fowl, fish, and vegetation, then they held some authority over this reserve. As God
was to human, so human was to beast. The beast was to fear
humans. As Genesis says, man was given "dominion over the
fish of the sea and the fowl of the air, and over the cattle and
over all the earth, and over every creeping thing that creepeth
upon the earth."

The not-so-subtle shift from stewardship to dominion was
achieved partly with the help of the Christian millenarian eschatology, the once fervently held hope that the second coming was

imminent. With this central tenet of Christian cosmology, it was almost natural for the believer to view the earth as simply a temporary way station, both for the individual soul on its way to the afterlife and for all inhabitants of the earth. As such, it simply did not matter what happened here for all this was vanity.

The result was that the Christian came to believe, as the pagan before him believed, that he could do basically what he pleased with animals, putting them to whatever use he deemed expedient in the furtherance of God's (read "man's") will. This use included everything from beast of burden to companion-pet to being consumed for food, as we saw fit. Sometimes the same animal fulfilled all three uses at different points in its life. At any rate, the transition from stewardship to dominion was marked by a corresponding upwardly mobile shift in man's own status vis-à-vis animals—from that of manager to de facto owner.

Even owners, however, observe certain constraints on the use to which they put their property. It was only with the rise of modern science and philosophy that the relationship between people and animals became increasingly estranged, and by which the animal came to be the object of systematic exploitation on our part. I am not speaking, for the moment, about modern scientific experimentation on animals, whether this be genuine medical experimentation or cosmetic toxicity testing. The Christian might have seen her way clear to similarly dispose of her animal charges had she available the instruments and science for doing so. Rather, the move to exploitation came with the rise of certain new theories involving the philosophy of mind and modern views about the status of animals' mental states.

With the ascent of modern scientific theory, particularly recent advances in medicine and physiology, eighteenth-century scientists and philosophers came to believe that all animal behavior (and some extended this to humans as well) could be explained in terms of mechanistic physical causes. We could explain all behavior in terms of movements of the muscles. These movements themselves were viewed to occur in accordance with the laws of physics and physiology, a result of impulses emanating from the brain and through the nervous system. The impulses in the brain were themselves seen as a function of complex

neuroelectrical processes, along with the release of various neu-
rotransmitters and other chemicals within the brain. While the
eighteenth-century scientist certainly did not understand all this
in its complexity, he did possess enough knowledge to be able
to predict that such processes would be so understood at a later
day. As such, he came to believe that all animal behavior could
be explained in terms of physical causes.

The emerging mechanistic worldview came to view animals
(and, again, sometimes humans) as extremely sophisticated
machines, but only machines. There was no place left for the
concept of mind or for such mental constructs as thinking, feeling, willing, desiring, believing, intending, and so on. All these
could be explained away as forms of unnecessary mental language. All behavior, after all, could be adequately described in
terms of physical processes in the brain and the body. While consciousness in humans posed a strange and difficult problem for
the new worldview—what function does consciousness have if
we would have performed all our behavior in the exact same
fashion without it?—the modern scientist completely overlooked
the problem of consciousness in the case of animals. Animals
were merely machines. Moreover, unlike the human machine,
animals did not even possess consciousness. As the philosopher
Descartes maintained, animals were mere "thoughtless brutes,"
incapable even of feeling or of sentience in the most primitive
form.

What followed as the result of this worldview were some of
the most brutal experiments ever performed upon animals, all
undertaken in the belief that animals were nonconscious machines. Thus, in order to observe the flow of blood or the functions of organs, scientists such as La Metrie engaged in vivi-
section experiments in which dogs were nailed by all four paws
onto boards, cut open without anesthetic and left in such conditions until future experiments, or until the animal died. The howl-
ing, crying, and evasive movements on the part of the poor
creatures were viewed not as expressions of genuine pain—the
animal was a nonconscious machine, after all—but merely as
survival mechanisms of the physical organism that outwardly
resembled our own real expressions of pain.

Such experimentation subsided, perhaps at least partially as the result of the experiments themselves. As vivisectionists came to see the overall physiological similarity between animals and humans, they may have begun to doubt their assumptions concerning animal consciousness. At any rate, the late eighteenth century was witness as other thinkers began to argue for improved treatment of animals. In 1776, the first animal rights treatise appeared in England, "A Dissertation on the Duty of Mercy and Sin of Cruelty to Brute Animals," authored by Rev. Humphrey Primatt. A few years later, the English utilitarian philosopher Jeremy Bentham began to argue for better treatment of animals.

During the eighteenth and nineteenth centuries, calls for greater respect for animals, when they occurred at all, were typically predicated not on some notion of animal rights—the idea of *human* rights was new enough—but upon either a general sense of mercy toward animals as sentient creatures or upon the idea that people's cruelty toward animals was bad for *people*. Immanuel Kant, for example, argued that cruelty to animals made us more cruel to one another. Still many other philosophers of the period continued to find often nebulous reasons for completely overlooking the interests of animals. The German idealist Hegel, for example, argued that animals "have no right to their life because they do not will it," meaning that they do not self-consciously desire their own continued existence.

Even among proponents of animal rights, animals were still far from regarded as individuals worthy of respect unto themselves, as creatures not very different from ourselves. Perhaps the greatest step in the direction of bridging the psychological gulf between humans and animals came after 1859, the year in which Darwin published his *Origin of Species*. It was only with the theory of evolution and the idea that humans are descended from animals, that we began to recognize that human beings are not so different from animals, after all.

Finally, with the exception of various anti-vivisectionist groups that were active throughout the early part of the twentieth century, little movement occurred in the develpment of our ideas concerning animals. It was only with the advent of the 1970s that philosophers again began to take up in earnest the question of animal rights.[3]

The Utilitarian Case for the
Protection of Animals

In the previous chapter, we saw that what makes one course of action better than another for the utilitarian is that the better course produces more pleasure or alleviates more pain, on balance, than any other course of action. But exactly *whose* pleasure is it that counts? Does only human pleasure matter in the hedonic calculus or is the pain and pleasure of animals to be factored into the equation as well?

Since it is the production of pleasure and the avoidance of pain that are viewed by the utilitarian to be equivalent to the goodness and badness of actions, respectively, there is no room on utilitarian grounds for distinguishing human from animal pleasure. Pleasure is pleasure, whether it is experienced by humans or other animals. Thus, utilitarianism requires that the interests of other animals be taken into account. Given that other animals experience pleasure and pain, humans cannot live at the expense of other animals, or by ignoring their interests as creatures who, like us, suffer.

The utilitarian case for animal rights focuses on three aspects of our maltreatment of animals. First, the living conditions under that farm animals and experimental animals are kept are abysmal. These animals typically live in desperately cramped and dangerously unclean living conditions, are not properly fed or exercised, are shot up with hormones and other chemicals that render animals seriously ill through much of their lives, are castrated, debeaked, force-molted, branded, and, in a veritable plethora of other ways, seriously abused and exploited. More will be said of these conditions shortly. Second, the utilitarian focuses upon the way in which the animals are killed. Despite so-called "humane slaughter" rules, the conditions leading to, and manner of, execution of these animals are shocking. Third, the utilitarian looks to the lost pleasure of these animals—that is, the pleasure they would have experienced had they been permitted to live normal life spans rather than the pitifully short lives modern factory farm animals live. When all of these factors are weighed together, it is clear that the limited pleasure that humans receive from eating meat is outweighed a hundredfold by the suffering endured by animals in order to secure this inhumane pleasure.

Moreover, not only is all this suffering preventable by adoption of a vegetarian diet, but no human pleasure is lost in the long run by doing so. Much of the pleasure that is derived from meat eating is the result of enculturation. People grow up accustomed to the taste of meat. Some, though not many, experience the transition from meat eating to vegetarianism as a privation, a loss of pleasure, because of the yearning for this taste.[4] But if vegetarianism were to become widely accepted, the next generation would grow up under vastly different conditions. No such feeling of privation would occur. When one factors in the health benefits inherent in vegetarianism (see chapter 3), it is clear that, from a utilitarian standpoint, the vegetarian diet is preferable *even from the standpoint of humans, ignoring for the moment the total prevention of animal suffering.* When one includes the suffering experienced by animals at the hands of modern agribusiness, however, the call for an end to meat eating becomes downright compelling. Let us take a few moments to detail exactly the extent to which animals suffer on the modern factory farms.

We begin with the chicken. From the very earliest step in the process of producing layer hens, death marks the process. Half the crop of newly hatched chicks—the males—are killed at birth because they produce neither eggs nor a high enough quality of meat. The male chicks are unceremoniously thrown into large plastic garbage bags where they suffocate or are crushed under the weight of their similarly condemned fellows.

With the application of modern industrial methods to the factory farm, farmers soon learned that it was cost-efficient to store their chickens indoors. The development of the use of vitamins A and D made it unnecessary for the hens to exercise or be exposed to natural sunlight. This permitted farmers to stuff four to five hens in cages with a twelve by eighteen inch floor size (roughly the size of a dinner tray.) (The birds are cheaper than the wire mesh cages.) In such cramped conditions, hens begin to peck at each other, often pecking other hens to death. In order to prevent this, farmers began using debeaking machines. The hen is held up to a machine with a sharp blade that saws off its beak. (It should be noted here that the beak is not an unfeeling appendage. The experience of debeaking is not greatly different from sawing off the nose of a human being.)

The overcrowding in these cramped cages also leads to the spread of disease among hens. Sulfa drugs and antibiotics are used, often in very high doses, to combat this. (The effects of these drugs when consumed by humans will be discussed in chapter 3). After a year or two in such conditions, egg production wanes. In order to increase egg production, layer hens are force molted. Forced-molting consists of placing hens in completely dark rooms without food or water for a period of a number of days. This process is effective only one or two times after which the hen is spent. And how is the hen rewarded for her few years of service once egg production falls below levels that make housing and feeding her no longer profitable? She is summarily sent to food processors that grind her up into soup stock or other consumer foods.

What becomes of the other (usually the smaller) female chicks who are not converted into layer hens? They are similarly caged, debeaked, injected with antibiotics and other drugs, and fattened on an unappetizing admixture of grain, sewage waste, and sawdust for eight weeks. After this short life, some four billion of these birds go to market each year in the United States alone.

The pig is perhaps the most unfairly maligned animal to be put to the service of mankind. The pig is as intelligent as the dog, is good-natured, and, given the proper environment, is a clean animal. These reasons make clear why pigs have recently become popular as pets. The pig on the factory farm is another matter, however. Within two weeks of birth, around weaning time, the male pig is wrestled down and castrated without anesthetic. Pigs spend their very short lives of roughly twenty weeks (they have a normal lifespan of about ten years) indoors in crowded pens with slatted floors that preclude the use of adequate bedding. Sows are confined to narrow pens that do not permit them to walk or turn around. There is only enough room to eat, drink, stand, or lie down, always with her teats exposed for the baby pigs. If the way in which the pig is forced to live is abysmal, the way in which it dies is worse. One commentator describes the scene as the pigs are herded to their deaths as follows:

The pen narrows like a funnel; the drivers behind urge the pigs forward, until one at a time they climb onto the moving ramp . . . Now they scream, never having been on such a ramp, smelling the smells they smell ahead . . . it was a frightening experience seeing their fear.[5]

What becomes of the pig after this is clear enough. The pigs' fate is to have an eight-inch long pin fired into their foreheads at point-blank range. Their blood and guts will spill forth on the killing floor, their carcasses will be stripped and carved and chopped during a process that, although it is governed by "humane slaughter" laws, can be nothing other than gross and brutal. [6]

The killing process for cows is described still more plainly by Jeremy Rifkin in *Beyond Beef*:

After being fattened to their "ideal" weight of 1,100 pounds, the mature steers are herded into giant truck trailers, where they are cramped together without room to move. Because the journey to the slaughter-house is often a rough and brutal one, animals frequently fall and are trampled upon inside the trucks, suffering broken legs or pelvises. Unable to rise, these animals are known as "downers". . . . The cattle are transported for hours a day . . . without rest or nourishment and frequently without water. At the end of their journey, intact animals are deposited in holding pens. . . . [Downers] are chained by their broken legs and dragged from the truck onto the loading ramp to await their turn for slaughter. . . . [U]pon entry, [intact animals] are stunned by a pneumatic gun. As each animal sinks to its knees, a worker quickly hooks a chain onto a rear hoof, and the animal is mechanically hoisted from the platform and hung upside down from the slaughterhouse floor. Men in blood-soaked gowns, handling long knives, slit each steer's throat, thrusting the blade deeply into the larynx for a second or two, then quickly withdrawing the knife, severing the jugular vein and carotid artery in the process. Blood spurts out over the workstation, splattering the workers and equipment.[7]

Such is the lot of animals destined and doomed to be consumed by human beings.

It was this ultramodern form of automated brutality that led in the 1970s to a new wave of concern on the part of philosophers and activists for the interests of animals. The Australian utilitarian philosopher Peter Singer was perhaps the first both to chronicle the plight of animals on the modern factory farm and to cast their interests into the form of utilitarian moral theory. Singer published *Animal Liberation* in 1975. What followed was a groundswell of reaction, both positive and by way of defense of the various uses of animals. By most accounts, the book is responsible for rekindling the modern animal rights movement.

The utilitarian argument for vegetarianism made by Singer and others is overwhelming. The maltreatment and slaughter of billions of animals a year amounts to an almost incomprehensible amount of "negative utility" (i.e., pain) experienced by animals. Nor is it a response that many of these animals would never have existed were it not for our meat-eating habits. No one has the right to bring any sentient creature into the world for the purpose of abusing it. To cast this response in utilitarian terms, there comes a point where the positive utility of existence is outweighed by the negative utility endemic of the manner of existence. In plainer words, the conditions of life may become so harsh, brutal, and burdensome, as they are for the modern factory farm animal, that it would be preferable, from that animal's standpoint, never to have lived at all. This objection is taken up at greater length in chapter 6.

Because of the sheer force of the utilitarian argument, numerous philosophers have attempted to defend meat-eating against the utilitarian attack. As one defender of the status quo candidly admits, if some way out is not discovered, "we would surely be headed for vegetarianism."[8] The preferred method by way of responding to the utilitarian case is to downgrade the pleasure and pain of animals vis-à-vis humans. One way of doing this is to argue that animals have no sense of the future and, thus, that their loss of life means less to them than does our loss of life. Later in this chapter, we will consider the question of animal intelligence. The status of the mental world of animals is a matter of some controversy but, undoubtedly, humans have underestimated animals' awareness of their lives. Suffice it to say for now that this argument is made without any knowledge of how various animals perceive the world, or what their mental dispositions are regarding their future existence.

Moreover, the objection that animal pleasure is less important than human pleasure because animals do not anticipate their futures is predicated upon an inaccurate account of utilitarian theory. Even if it were true that certain animals do not have the mental capacity necessary to foresee their future existence, this is irrelevant from the standpoint of utilitarianism. The utilitarian gives weight to the experience of pleasure (or, in the case of more modern versions of utilitarianism, satisfying a preference). The fact that one species can foresee its utility at a certain future time while another cannot does not render the utility to the latter creature less valuable. Thus, this objection misses the central point of utilitarianism.

Another attempt to "downgrade" animal pleasure is to argue that animals' experiences of pleasure are not as valuable to them because animals are incapable of judging and articulating their feelings of pleasure. This argument similarly misunderstands utilitarian theory. First, inability to "articulate one's pleasure" has nothing to do with its intrinsic value. There undoubtedly exist humans who, for a variety of physical reasons, are unable to articulate their pleasure for example, the stroke victim who cannot talk—and yet this is no reason to downgrade the value of pleasure to the stroke victim. Nor is it relevant, even if it is true, that animals cannot evaluate and make second-order judgments about their first-order feelings of pleasure. As we shall see in the following sections, animals move toward and obviously appreciate pleasurable experiences as much as do humans. Even if they cannot "form judgments" of these experiences, this is irrelevant to utilitarian theory for similar reasons that left the first objection inappropriate: what is valuable to the utilitarian is the experience of pleasure, not forming judgments about pleasurable experiences.

Other philosophers raise a number of alternative objections to the utilitarian account, most of which are attacks on utilitarian theory itself. For example, Fox argues that if it is difficult to quantify pleasure states in humans (see the discussion of the utilitarian's position regarding happiness in chapter 1) it is even more difficult in animals.[9] The response to this objection is simple: while it may be difficult to place a numerical value on the pleasurable and painful states of animals in order to compare them with similar states in humans, the amount of negative utility in terms of the horrible living conditions under which animals live, the way in which they die, and their lost lives far outweighs our pleasure in eating animals. Who would deny, with a straight face, that the exploitation and slaughter of billions of animals a year

in the United States alone more than outweighs whatever pleasure is derived from the consumption of the same animals by
two hundred million or so humans? In short, how could there be
more pleasure for humans in eating animals than that which is
lost to them in giving up their lives, particularly when there are
over ten times as many animals that die each year as there are
humans consuming them?

Finally, Fox seems to believe that the utilitarian objection to
killing animals can be met by more "humane" and painless ways
of killing than exist today.[10] Again, this may ameliorate the conditions under which farm animals die, but it is completely unre-
sponsive both to the horrible conditions under which they are
made to live and the lost utility in virtue of the future lives cut
short (often radically, as in the case of the pig).

Concerning the case for vegetarianism, the defender of meat
eating is left without a leg to stand on, whether we look to classical utilitarian theory or to commonsense notions of mercy at
the suffering endured by animals. In the end, it is the suffering
that the meat eating philosopher, apparently with some sense of
guilt, attempts to justify, although vainly:

> It remains that we think suffering is a bad thing, no matter whose.
> But although we think so, we do not think it is so bad as to require
> us to become vegetarians. Here, by "we" of course, I mean most of
> us. And what most of us think is that although suffering is too
> bad and it is unfortunate for animals that they are turned into
> hamburger at a tender age, we nevertheless are justified on the
> whole in eating them.[11]

In the end, the philosopher responsible for this quote abandons
his case to an appeal to what "most of us" think. But if this
were the final criterion for moral debate, there would be no need
for philosophy in the first place.

The Sinking Ship and the Veil of Ignorance: Contractarianism and the Moral Status of Animals

Imagine the following scenario: You are the captain of a steam-
liner that has sunk after hitting an iceberg in the North Atlantic.

You now find yourself at sea in a lifeboat with twenty-six passengers—twenty-five people and one dog. The lifeboat is extremely crowded. While you have enough provisions aboard to last until rescue, which is likely to take place within a week, the lifeboat has one passenger too many. The boat is taking on water and you have determined that the lifeboat will only stay afloat if one of the passengers is jettisoned. As you are captain, the decision as to which passenger to sacrifice falls to you. You also, however, have been an ardent lover of animals and a believer in animal rights. As a manifestation of your strong belief, you are a vegetarian. The question with which you are now faced is: Do you throw the dog over first?

Disregard, for the moment, the legal implications: sacrificing the person will likely lead to a charge of manslaughter, if not murder, while throwing the dog overboard would be completely justified by the legal defense of necessity. This is because the law still regards an animal as property rather than as a life. Property can be sacrificed for the common good; human lives cannot.

Animal rights activists, vegetarians, and others are faced with the problem of prioritizing the interests of humans and animals in a manner similar to that which was elaborated in the lifeboat scenario. The dilemma they face is as follows: If the animal rights supporter takes the position that the life of a dog has exactly the same value as that of a human, the position appears extreme and—to many, including some vegetarians and animal rights activists—counterintuitive. Are all animals equal? If it would be wrong to throw a dog overboard, what about a chicken, a mollusk, or an insect? Such a conclusion appears to ignore the very real differences between these species, both physically and mentally. Thus, it is likely that few supporters of animal rights would defend what seems like such a radical proposition, which we might call "pan-species egalitarianism."

On the other hand, if the vegetarian admits that there are relevant differences such that the dog in our example should be sacrificed before any person is, she fears that she may be opening herself up to attacks of the variety: "So even *you* think it is all right to kill animals in some situations; how, then, can you say that we shouldn't eat meat?" The vegetarian suspects that, by admitting that animals are not completely equal in status to humans, she will have lost the moral foundation for the case for vegetarianism. But this is simply not true. The fact that an animal may be sacrificed in one situation (where the survival of people is at stake) does not entail that *any* justification (e.g., the taste for animal flesh) warrants eating meat.

Of course, the problem can always be further complicated. While a dog may be sacrificed so that a person may live, should a hundred dogs die so that the same person should live? A million dogs? What if the person is a ninety-year-old terminally ill patient who is comatose and has no possibility of regaining consciousness? Should this same number be sacrificed for other human interests—that is, interests less compelling than the survival of a person? Every year in the United States alone, we put to death seventeen million stray cats and dogs rather than bear the expense of caring for them, a strong endorsement of the view that even lesser humans interests have priority over animal lives.[12] This same position reaches its (almost) logical extreme in the killing and injuring of animals in large numbers for the development and testing of human conveniences such as cosmetics.

This variety of line-drawing problem is the sort that has philosophers pulling their hair out while simultaneously constituting the stock-in-trade of the law professor. They are designed to test the limits of a principle. Very few principles are absolute in the sense that they admit no objection or exception. Still, where should the line be drawn in the case of our obligations to animals?

As a primary matter, it should be noticed that these problems are not particular to this issue; they arise even in the context where we are weighing human lives against human lives, as in the decision whether to go to war. But how are such decisions to be made? One answer is to weigh, in utilitarian fashion, the number of lives saved, subtracting from this the number of lives lost, by following different courses of action. By this utilitarian theory, the course of action that preserves the most lives is generally the best. We saw in the last section that the utilitarian case for vegetarianism is strong. But if, for reasons discussed in the last chapter, one finds utilitarianism unsatisfactory as the foundation for a moral theory, are there any alternatives?

Modern forms of deontological thought offer still other ways of determining whether human interests take priority over those of animals, and whether this priority is absolute. One deontological approach that philosophers have been reexploring recently is called "contractarianism." John Rawls's 1971 work, *A Theory of Justice*, one of the most important books to be written this century on the subject of social philosophy, follows this contractarian model.

The contractarian approach provides as follows: Social and political relations in the real world are usually (perhaps always) unjust and inequitable. Groups that are able to secure to themselves a certain amount of power are able to hold down still other groups, such as minorities, the weak, and the disenfranchised. Thus, power relationships as they exist tend to become unfair, even if they started out fairly at some point early in that society's history. Thus, we need a way to determine which social arrangements and relationships are fair and which are not. The only way to make the determination of what is truly fair, is to attempt to find out what these people *would have agreed to* before they took on their social roles, without the benefit of the social and political biases inherent in the real world. Rawls elaborates a device for making this determination, which he calls "the veil of ignorance."

The veil of ignorance operates basically as follows: imagine putting everyone who is to live in a society together in a giant cosmic convention hall where they will negotiate the terms of the "social contract" that is to govern all social relationships. Everyone possesses general knowledge about the conditions of the world—what it takes to live, which living conditions are preferable to which, and so on. What the members do not know, because of the veil of ignorance, is where in society they she will wind up. (Indeed, they do not even know which sex they will be since this may also skew the results.) Each citizen-negotiator is ignorant about whether he or she will turn up wealthy or poor, a member of a minority group or one of the dominant class, heterosexual or homosexual, healthy or weak.

Rawls argues that, in this state, which he calls the "original position," totally ignorant of what is to be one's lot in life—and with all of the built-in bias to result from this knowledge eliminated—citizens will arrive at the social agreement that is fairest because each party wants to maximize his or her social advantages no matter where he or she may end up in society. Specifically, the agreement would serve to maximize everyone's freedom and to permit the better off, those who turn up in favorable social positions, to pursue their fortunes *but only if such arrangements are also to the advantage of the less fortunate.* Thus, for Rawls, inequality is not necessarily unjust. Rather, inequality is only unfair if it is at the expense of others, or if it does not also benefit others. For example, before giving the rich a tax break, it must be demonstrated that doing so will help the least advantaged as well, for example, by providing more jobs.

A great deal more could be said about Rawls's theory but the broad essentials have been mentioned here. The fundamental point is that, when placed in the original position, rational beings will create social arrangements that will benefit all, even if not all equally. To put it another way, no rule would be adopted that would permit one person or group to benefit *at the expense of* another person or group.

It has occurred to a number of philosophers that the veil of ignorance could be extended even further, beyond the domain of humans, to include all animals.[13] Suppose all animals, human and otherwise, convened a similar convention, all shrouded in the veil of ignorance such that no one knew where he or she would land in society, or *whether* he or she would land in human society. Where each party does not know whether she will turn up a human or an animal, what sort of a relationship would be created between humans and animals? What kinds of obligations would humans have toward animals?

Following similar reasoning as that employed by the parties in Rawls's original position, the signatories to this new, trans species social contract would permit no rule that would benefit some at the unnecessary expense of others. Since these parties would have access to all general knowledge necessary to making their decisions, and this would include a general understanding of nutritional knowledge, they would know that meat eating was not necessary to the survival of humans. Further, since each party would also face a great possibility of winding up an animal, human vegetarianism would be the obvious response to the question of diet. It would be the most rational response by the party who is not certain whether he will end up human or animal, pursuer or pursuee, the eater or the eaten.

Note here that a different agreement might certainly take place if an omnivorous diet were necessary to human survival. In this event, all parties might take their chances, leaving open the possibility for human survival even with the risk they might turn out to be a cow. Even here, however, the parties would sanction only the *least amount* of carnage necessary to maintain human survival. Eating animal meat for the pleasure of it would remain a breach of the social contract.

Numerous objections have been raised to the contractarian analysis of animal rights. At least one defender of omnivorism agrees that vegetarianism would be the result of such a trans-species agreement but argues that it is not proper to extend the social contract to animals because they are not rational beings.[14] As such, this philosopher follows Kant in limiting membership in the moral community to those deemed to be rational.

Two responses are in order here. First, it need not be a requirement of contractarian theory that every creature living under the conditions of the social contract must be rational. Many of those in Rawls's original position might turn out to be children, the mentally ill, the mentally handicapped, or others who fall outside the scope of what we might for the moment call "rational." Yet they are protected by the social contract. What is important is not that each creature *wind up* a rational being, but that the rules that form the social contract *are negotiated by parties in the original position who are rational* and who do not know whether they will wind up as a "rational" human being or as a (presumably) "irrational" animal. (Questions concerned with comparisons of the mental and moral status of animals, infants, and the mentally handicapped will be taken up in the last section of this chapter.)

Second, as we shall see in the following sections, certain species of animals do exhibit behaviors characteristic of what we call "rationality." While the level of intellectual ability obviously varies from species to species, animals do engage in the animal equivalent of human thinking, desiring, and deliberation, among others. Indeed, as we shall see, they sometimes engage

in actions that, if performed by humans, we would deem morally heroic.

Modern contractarianism does not require that humans and
animals are morally equivalent in every respect. A contractarian
model would minimally entail vegetarianism, however, and might
very well require other human concessions, from the standpoint
of the status quo, to animals. But humans could still take priority in cases where human survival was at stake and where the
costs in terms of animal interests and lives was not unduly excessive.

Do Pigs Think?: The Case for
Animal Intelligence and Animal Culture

Other varieties of deontological thought concentrate not on hy-
pothetical agreements, as with contractarianism, but on more
general principles having to do with an animal's ability to experience, think, desire, and have other mental states which entitle
that animal to protection. For example, the deontological animal
rights philosophy of Tom Regan uses the "subject of a life" criterion—any creature who is sentient, who experiences, who is
the subject of a life, has a right to that life.[15] The idea is that,
what makes life precious is the *experience* of it; it is consciousness that gives life value and that makes taking life morally
wrong.

This explains why eating plants is not morally objectionable.
Plants do not have nervous systems and, though they may
respond to certain external stimuli (growing toward sunlight,
withering when placed in close proximity to loud music, etc.),
there is no physiological apparatus (e.g. no brain and nervous
system) by which they can *experience* any of this as conscious
entities. In short, the plant reacts physically but does not
subjectively experience this physical reaction. Most basically,
plants do not have a "mental life" in any relevant sense of the
term. (See chapter 6 for an extended discussion of line-drawing
problems and the moral difference between eating plants and
animals.)

We saw earlier in this chapter that some scientists once held
a similar view of animals. They believed that the physical reac-

tions of animals were not accompanied by feelings, experiences of pain, or other mental activity; animals were, according to this view, merely machines. What changed their view about this was the discovery that the physical systems of animals—their brains and nervous systems—were not so very different from our own.

In this section, I will argue that the mental life of various mammals and other animals are not greatly different from our mental lives. Yes, it is true that animals do not have the same *intellectual* capacity as we do—they are not capable of doing complex mathematical operations, they have not sent one of their own to the moon, nor have they made medical and scientific discoveries—but, in other respects, animals experience life in a way very similar to us. Two kinds of evidence will be examined to make our case here. First, we will look at physiological evidence of our similarity to animals. Second, and perhaps more interestingly, we will discuss stories of animal behavior that demonstrate that animals think, feel, experience emotions and desires, and make decisions.

Higher mammals such as dogs, cats, pigs, and others share with humans a brain structure consisting of three components: the brain stem, the "middle brain" or limbic system (which, together with the brain stem is known as the "old brain"), and the "new brain," or neocortex. The brain stem is responsible for monitoring and regulating a wide variety of physiological processes such as breathing, heartbeat, and the hormonal system, along with performing a wide variety of primitive behavior such as hunting, eating, and self-defense; it is the most primitive portion of the brain, evolutionarily and physiologically. Reptiles and many sea creatures possess only this portion of the brain.

The middle brain or limbic system is responsible for and generally associated with the experience of emotion. Less developed mammals such as the kangaroo, which have developed to the middle brain stage, have limbic systems very similar to our own. Our emotional lives must be similar to animals at this stage though, of course, our emotional lives are also influenced by the thought patterns of the neocortex. The neocortex is the portion of the brain associated with thinking and, in humans, with rationality, language capacity, and a number of higher intellectual functions.

At the risk of oversimplifying just a bit, the mental life of human beings can be viewed as a layering of three different levels of mental process: the monitoring processes and stimulus-response behavior of the brain stem, the emotional states associated with the limbic system, and the thought processes of the neocortex. Undoubtedly, each new level of development in turn influences and modifies the level of experience characteristic of the previous stage; for example, emotion will accompany, and perhaps even modify, stimulus-response behavior. Similarly, the development of the neocortex permits us to think about our emotions, a development that can modify the emotional experience itself. This three-level layering of mental experience is shared by humans and more-developed mammals alike.

What distinguishes humans from other animals is the extent of development of the neocortex. Humans have a brain-to-body ratio six times higher than what would be expected based on animals of a similar size.[16] Much of this is due to the development of the neocortex. It is this ratio that scientists look to as determinative in inter species comparisons of intelligence. Thus, though an elephant has an absolute brain mass almost three times greater than humans—4 kilograms to 1.5 kilograms for humans—the even-greater difference in weight between the elephant and humans entails a much smaller brain-to-body ratio for elephants. It should be noted that dolphins also have an "expected brain size" six times the size of similarly sized animals. This supports what we already know through our own interaction with dolphins—that they are extremely intelligent mammals, perhaps with as much intellectual potential as humans. Whales appear to be similarly endowed with a brain-to-body ratio matching that of humans.[17]

Genetically, as humans, we are not far removed from our biological ancestors. Evolutionarily, the human line split off from the gorilla-chimpanzee line only eight to ten million years ago, at roughly the same time black, brown, and sun bears divided.[18] African apes (chimpanzees, pygmy chimpanzees, and gorillas) are closer to humans genetically than they are to the Asian apes such as the orangutan or the gibbon. Most compellingly, our ultimate genetic blue-print, the DNA sequence, is 97.5 percent similar to that of our closest sub hominoid relative, the chimpanzee.[19] Genetically, very little distinguishes us from animals we often cage, exploit, and, in some cultures, eat.

The intellectual capacities of various monkeys are the subject of numerous studies and anecdotal reports. There is one report of a domesticated chimp who can plow with a tractor, mow lawns manually or with a riding mower, build fences, hay cattle, bait its own hook and fish, eat with a fork and knife, and use the toilet when it is in the house.[20] Vervet monkeys display a wide variety of complex intellectual, social, and communicative skills. They appear to be able to distinguish true from false states of affairs as when they know that a particular alarm call is a mistake.[21] They also obviously understand social relationships and seem to be able to put themselves "in the shoes of" other animals. For example, when the cries of an infant monkey were played on a tape recorder, other vervet monkeys responded by looking to the infant's mother.

Other accounts also suggest the vervet's understanding of social relationships, along with the propensity found in certain human groups for one party to hold responsible the relatives of another who has offended him. For example, after a fight between two monkeys, the first monkey is more likely to threaten the close relatives of the second monkey. And even the first monkey's relatives may react in this way. We see in this behavior the obvious antecedents of clan warfare.

Animals may also engage in elaborate devices in order to avoid punishment, a fact that makes clear both their understanding of social hierarchies and relations and their anticipation of possible future events, including responses by others. In one study, a young female baboon placed herself in a position where she could see the dominant male, but ensuring that the male could not see her grooming a younger male, an act that often leads to retaliation by the older male. In another study, a chimp was made aware of a large store of bananas. The chimp studiously avoided looking toward the position of the bananas so as not to tip off the other chimps to his cache. He subsequently hoarded the bananas for himself.[22] These behaviors suggest not only thought on the part of these animals, but creative anticipation, intention, and the ability to carry through a plan.

Finally, chimpanzees are capable of logical inference in the strict-est sense of the term. For example, studies indicate that they understand the transitive relationship: they understand that where one amount (A) is greater than a second amount (B), and where the second amount (B) is greater than a third amount (C), the first amount (A) will also be greater than the third amount (C). Chimps are similarly able to engage in simple forms of reasoning by analogy. They have also demonstrated their comprehension that the amount of liquid in a container is conserved despite changes in container size. Human children do not master this operation until roughly the age of seven.[23]

Nor are human mental and emotional states different from those of most other mammals, including the domestic farm animals upon which we routinely feed. This is revealed not only by the behavior of these animals in their responses to external stimuli (e.g., frustration leads to more aggressive behavior) but in the physiological states underlying such behavior. For example, the neurochemistry of certain emotional states (such as anxiety and stress) vary little even between mice and men. Dogs have electrical brain activity, as measured by the EEG machine, which is almost identical to humans. Dogs experience waking, sleeping, and REM sleep with patterns very similar to humans. Indeed, dogs even daydream.[24] It requires no leap of logic to assume that dogs fantasize about desired objects, an activity formerly reserved to humans and human imagination.

If the mental life of dogs is similar in these fundamental ways to our own mental existence, so too, must be the experience of pigs, sheep, and cows. Little distinguishes these animals from dogs, neurologically. They, too, must desire, form attachments to other animals, remember their fellows, and interact socially in a variety of complex ways with humans and other animals.

This is borne out by studies on sheep. Sheep are social animals who form strong familial bonds with other sheep. The need for attachment is so compelling that lambs will become attached to other animals if the mother sheep is not present and if the two animals are confined together. In one study, lambs became attached to dogs, followed them around and became distressed when separated from the dogs.[25] These emotional responses cannot be distinguished from human feelings by calling the former "instinctual" and the latter "human," or by calling animal attraction "imprinting" while human attachment is described as "bonding." The human infant and the lamb respond in the same ways to separation from others. In either case, the behavior is the same. It is implausible to suppose that the *feeling* of distress or separation anxiety should be very different between animal and humans.

Sheep also have excellent memories. After months of separation from one researcher, bighorn sheep came willingly to the researcher, an indication both of their natural affection and their sharp memories. Sheep also make commonsense inferences about the world around them—inferences that, if made by a human, might merit the description "logical." For example, when one researcher hid from sight, "the sheep did not search the area where he had disappeared, but instead attempted to intercept him at the place where he should have been had he continued on a straight line, a fact which requires insight rather than mere association."[26] Pigs undoubtedly have similar capacities and experience thoughts and emotions of the same variety. It is, perhaps, our taste for pork, ham, lamb, and mutton that makes our general ignorance of the facts concerning the intelligence of these animals so culpably widespread.

The human animal has long sought ways to distinguish itself from other animals. Aristotle called man "the rational animal." As we have seen, however, other animals clearly evince telltale signs of rationality such as the making of logical inferences, reasoning by analogy, and various commonsense inferences. Next, we distinguished ourselves by our use of language. But "language" is employed by many species from the dance of the bee, which communicates information about the distance and location of food, to the use of sign language by chimpanzees. Apes particularly amazed researchers when they engaged in behaviors thought to be exclusively those of the human province: chimps created new words from old (e.g., combining the signs for "water" and "sweet," creating the new word "watersweet" as the designation for watermelon) and teaching this language to their young. While it is true that the linguistic capacities of chimps appear to be limited neurologically to a level similar to that of a two-year-old child, in other respects their development is much greater.

Next, we claimed the use of tools and implements as ours alone until we discovered that even some birds use tools.[27] Tool use is also common among many other animals, including the monkey who, for example, will use a bamboo reed to draw ants from an underground colony, licking them from the reed. Finally, we resolved to satisfy ourselves in our yearning for evolutionary distinction by claiming that only humans possess culture. This too, however, has proved to be a failed strategy. Matriarchal elephants, for example, retain information concerning dry season feeding grounds. This information is crucial to the survival of the group. This traditional knowledge, which is passed from one generation to the next and which is more important to elephants than to any other animal besides man, is precisely what we mean by "culture" when discussing human culture. Similarly, Richard Leakey and Roger Lewin write that "[a] troop of chimpanzees . . . has access to a pool of knowledge greater than any one individual would possess." This knowledge is passed from generation to generation and constitutes "the rudiments of culture."[28]

Animals engage in many of the same mental processes and social activities as humans. They think, desire, feel emotion, and, use tools and other implements. In some cases, they employ language in a varied array of social contexts. While humans may do all this in greater depth or with more complexity, the difference is one of degree, not kind.

With nowhere left to turn but within ourselves, modern man seeks distinction today in a more subtle way—in our claim to be the exclusive possessors of self-consciousness.

The Chimp That Would Be Human: Self-Awareness and the Moral Status of Animals

A number of other philosophers have argued that what essentially distinguishes the mental states of humans from those of other animals is that, while animals may be conscious, only humans are self-conscious. It is this self-consciousness that makes human beings special and that gives us alone a right to our lives.

What is meant, exactly, by self-consciousness is sometimes

not clear. Sometimes self-consciousness appears to mean the ability to have second-order mental states. A "second-order" mental state is a mental state about another (first-order) mental state. So, the ability to think about an emotion would be an example of a second-order state and would exemplify self-consciousness under this definition. The essential idea is that, if we can think about our mental states and emotions, we have an awareness of them and of ourselves that far transcends the animal who simply experiences, that is, who simply has first-order mental states, such as emotions, without being able to think about them.

Another sense of the term "self-consciousness" is the notion that we are aware of ourselves as separate entities in the world. This requires that we are aware, first, that we *exist*, second, that we *persist*—that we exist through time with a past and with a future—and, finally, that we distinguish ourselves from other beings in the world. Psychologists employ two tests to determine if children or animals possess self-consciousness in this sense. First, the child or animal must be able to recognize itself (in a mirror, for example) and, second, it must have the ability to make guesses about other people's feelings.[29] This second criterion demonstrates both that the subject understands that the other has feelings and is itself a separate self, and requires that the subject have sufficient self-insight that it can make reasonable guesses about the feelings of others.

There is undoubtedly some overlap between these two conceptions. The ability to make guesses about others' feelings requires a second-order awareness of one's own feelings. And having a second-order awareness of one's own feelings probably requires that one see oneself as a separate entity, distinct from others in the world.

Some philosophers and writers argue that animals do not possess this higher level of awareness known as self-consciousness. Even if they experience emotions, and even if they are capable of thinking thoughts, this view holds, they cannot think about these emotions or thoughts in second-order fashion. Alternatively, this view holds that animals are not aware of themselves as separate entities experiencing the world; they are rather like the newborn infant who has not yet distinguished self and world.

As such, all the world is experienced as part of one all-encom-passing experience.

Whether animals experience self-consciousness in either of these senses may depend upon the species in question. Chim-panzees appear to meet the previously mentioned tests. One fas-cinating account exists of a young, female chimp who was given the task of sorting photographs into two piles, one pile consist-ing of a variety of animals including dogs and horses, and the second pile consisting of people. Simply being able to perform this task successfully as she did demonstrates a high level of abstraction in that she was able to classify different kinds of animals as members of the same group while simultaneously distinguishing humans, sorting them into a separate group. But then came the real twist in the experiment: as the young chimp sorted through the pile, she came across a picture of herself. How did she respond? By placing it in the pile with the *other* hu-mans, of course![30] This is remarkable not only for the fact that she recognized herself, but because it demonstrates that she saw herself as a person, not as an animal.

Such experiments go a long way toward demonstrating that chimpanzees possess the self-consciousness ascribed only to hu-mans. The chimp in the last example met the first test of recog-nizing herself. And even less developed mammals appear to pass the second test consisting of anticipating the feelings or responses of others. For example, dogs and cats will often show displea-sure, frustration, or anger by inhibited bites that do not injure. This strongly suggests an awareness, on the part of the animal, of the human being as a separate entity.

Reluctant to accept the view that animals possess (second order) self-consciousness or even (first-order) simple conscious-ness, some have argued that animal behavior occurs in stimulus-response fashion. According to this behaviorist account, the dog who gently bites its master as a sign of displeasure is not react-ing to its master as a separate being, but rather, is simply react-ing to previous punishment where it bit too forcefully and was punished. Similarly, the dog who has stolen a steak from the dinner table is not reacting to its guilt or embarrassment after-ward; it simply seeks to avoid being punished when it looks sheepishly from its corner. In this fashion, even the most "human looking" animal behavior is reduced to a stimulus-response model: that is, animals do not have feelings such as guilt or anxiety, nor are they particularly cognizant of other animals and people as separate entities with feelings of their own; rather, they merely have been taught that a painful response may follow certain behavior.

This view is altogether too prevalent and, yet, is hopelessly inaccurate and unsupported by the evidence. First, of course, some psychologists say exactly the same thing about human behavior.[31] Notwithstanding the fact that we actually feel the feelings we experience such as guilt, love, anxiety, attachment, and so on, some behaviorist psychologists maintain that these feelings are functionally unimportant, that is, our guilt is not the cause of our doing the right thing; it is the response to past punishment that motivates our behavior. As such, guilt is merely a psychological side effect of our fear of punishment, for example.

Of course, if such a view could be seriously maintained with respect to humans, it is certain to be downright abused in the case of animals. With animals, the view goes one step further, holding not merely that feelings are unimportant, but that they do not exist at all. In reality, however, feelings are functional components of—*they have causal influence over*—both human and animal behavior. Nothing else can explain why some animals become obviously depressed, becoming listless and refusing to eat, when their master dies or leaves for a period of time. Nothing else can explain the outpouring of joy upon the return of this same master. Similarly, nothing else can explain the obvious fear of animals who watch as their fellows before them are slaughtered. In essence, the behavior is too much like our own to classify animals as "unfeeling machines."

The difference between humans and other animals is not that humans alone have (first-order) feelings and emotions, or that only humans have desires, or draw inferences or daydream or think certain thoughts. Perhaps all mammals and even some lower-order animals (e.g., chickens) have such experiences, though the depth and variety of these will vary with the level of evolutionary development. Nor are humans alone self-conscious. While the line between simple and self-consciousness is undoubtedly fuzzy and gradual, higher mammals exhibit many, if not all, of the characteristics of self-awareness. What higher animals such as the African apes, dolphins, and perhaps whales cannot do is to objectify and articulate their mental states as humans can. They cannot achieve the distance from their mental states that we can from ours by our use of language. It is our development of language, along with its reflexive effect upon the growth of the neocortex over the course of the past half-million years or so, that has resulted in the psychological acuity by which we, as humans, can objectify our mental states and, indeed, ourselves.

As for the less developed of the higher mammals—the dog, the pig, the sheep, and perhaps the cow—self-awareness is more shadowy still. These animals are certainly aware of themselves in the sense that they tailor their behavior to the responses of others, as when the poodle, fresh from a wash and haircut, prances proudly about. They also draw inferences about the behavior of others, responding accordingly, as when the pet pig drags its dish to its master when it is hungry. Whether pigs actually think about themselves in a more objective way, forming second-order mental judgments about their first-order mental states, is a matter of conjecture. In the end, however, why should this even matter? Why should we deny a right to life to an animal with the intelligence of a pig, for example—an animal that feels pain, experiences emotion, forms attachments, makes commonsense inferences about the world—predicating the right upon the capacity to form higher-order judgments about these feelings? The distinction appears ad hoc, an attempt to justify the status quo after the fact.

Some philosophers have argued that, in order to have any rights, including a right to life, the subject must first be a *moral agent*—it must be capable of making moral decisions. In the following section, we shall see that many animals may fit even this lofty criterion.

Rescue by Gorilla: Animals as Moral Agents

Animals appear to have feelings and reactions that, if they were to occur in the human context, would be described not only in "feeling" language, but also as character traits exhibiting moral virtue. Indeed, it is ironic that similar behavior is described in such radically different terms, depending upon whether it is a human or an animal that performs it. For example, geese mate for life. When a goose loses its lifelong mate, it shows signs of great distress; it searches wildly, seems to lose its normal sense of self-preservation, and sometimes dies soon thereafter. In a similar account, a scientist discovered two ducks, a male and a female, who were constantly together. Affectionately dubbed "John Duck" and "Mary Duck" by the scientist, the male led the female around, providing for her needs, feeding her, staying with her. On closer examination, it was discovered that the female duck was blind. Yet, her companion never abandoned her.[32] When humans show such devotion, it is called "love"; when geese or ducks do, it is called "instinct." In this way, we employ pseudo-scientific language to obscure important facts about the mental lives of animals.

Accounts of behavior among animals ranging from the merely cooperative to the altruistic to the outright heroic are legion. The following is only a representative sample of documented instances of such behavior.

Accounts of apes acting as moral agents—arbitrating disputes, forming partnerships, and protecting other animals are well known. In one interesting account, a dominant male gorilla played Solomon in settling a dispute between two females. The two females began to fight when the dominant female kidnapped the infant of the other female. Usually, the dominant male protected the dominant female. In this case, however, the male sided with the other female who had been wronged, breaking up the fight, restoring the infant to its mother, and pushing the dominant female away. Here, there simply is no other plausible description for the male gorilla's behavior except to say that the male acted as a moral agent, overlooking his ties with the perpetrator here, perhaps feeling sympathy for the other female, *and doing the right thing.*[33]

Stories of heroism among dolphins and whales are as widespread as they are popular. Some species of whales have been observed to aid not only members of their own species, but members of other species as well. There are similar accounts of dolphins circling humans, preventing shark attacks and, in September, 1978 off Auckland, New Zealand, the case of dolphins shepherding beached whales back to the open ocean after humans could do nothing to get the whales to return to sea.[34]

A Russian account from Tass describes another incident in the Black Sea in 1977. Dolphins sought the help of sailors in removing a young dolphin from a fishing net. The dolphins circled the ship until the sailors raised anchor, at which point the dolphins sped off, leading the sailors to their distressed fellow.[35] These stories are remarkable not only for what they say about the thought processes of these animals—the ability to jointly carry though a plan, their understanding that humans might be able to assist them, and so on—but for what it says about their commitment to other individuals. Again, if it were human behavior we were describing, terms such as "loyalty," "bravery," "tenacity" would not be in short supply.

Perhaps the most interesting story concerns a dolphin named Pelorus John who routinely guided ships through the rocky and dangerous French Pass off the coast of New Zealand. One day when Pelorus John made his appearance to guide an American ship, the *Penguin*, a drunk man aboard deck fired his gun at the dolphin, striking him. Pelorus John disappeared for a number of months and seaman supposed him dead. After some time, however, he reappeared, apparently healed, and resumed his old habit of guiding ships through the pass—that is, for all ships but the *Penguin*. He never again came near this ship. Some time after, the *Penguin* was wrecked in the same French Pass, and many of its passengers drowned.[36]

Nor are such heroics reserved to dolphins and apes. Stories of the devotion of dogs to their families are almost routine. In one such account from the small town of Euless, Texas, a two year-old boy wandered into the middle of a busy highway. His St. Bernard followed him and protected the boy, stopping cars and tying up traffic in both directions by barking and running around the child until the boy was removed from the street.

Even farm animals have played the role of hero. United Press International carried the story of Anthony Melton, a Houston, Texas, boy who wandered too far out into the middle of a pond and began to drown as his mother watched helplessly. The boy's pet pig, Priscilla, swam out to him. The boy was able to keep himself afloat long enough to grab the pig's leash. With the boy in tow, Priscilla swam back to shore.[37]

Heroic animal behavior of this variety simply cannot be explained without acknowledging that animals have an intelligence and a sensitivity that far exceeds our traditional view of them. Thinkers such as the respectable moral philosopher Joel Feinberg, who argue that animals lack a conscience—that animals simply fear reprisal—cannot account for acts such as those described here that go above and beyond the call of duty. With our recognition of animals as moral agents, surely the last obstacle to granting them full protection as individuals must fall.

Animals, Infants and the Mentally Handicapped: The Sanctity of Sentience as a Moral Criterion

If self-consciousness, intellectual capacity, or certain other technical abilities are viewed as essential to the superior moral status of human beings, such that only humans have a right to life in virtue of these abilities, what explains our protection of infants, the severely mentally ill, and the seriously mentally handicapped? It is at least a year before babies pass either of the two tests associated with self-consciousness. Nor can the human infant engage in any of the various intellectual skills that separate humans from animals. As Bentham said, a horse is more rational than a newborn infant. Similarly, the mentally disabled may be unable to perform even the simplest mental tasks. In the case of the autistic, it is not certain whether the subject distinguishes self and world at all, and in the case of the catatonic, from an external standpoint it does not appear that there is any subjective experience whatsoever. Still we protect these individuals, as we should. But why, or more appropriately, why not also protect animals?

It is in response to this question that the bonds of rationalization grow brittle, unable to support the intellectual house of cards that is the argument for our right to eat animals. While infants are *potentially* rational, and while potential rationality may give the infant a right to life, as some philosophers argue, this does little to advance the case of the irretrievably mentally handicapped. Nor is the claim that we simply ought to feel a bond to other humans, even if they lack these defining intellectual characteristics, as Fox argues in *The Case for Animal Experimentation*, relevant.[38] An exhortation to feel compassion for others who lack our intellectual gifts could be applied equally well to animals. At any rate, it becomes clear that Fox's principle for distinguishing human from animal—our autonomy and the ability to recognize autonomy in others—is only a rationalization. If we are obligated to protect the severely mentally handicapped and if the handicapped fail this test, then clearly this test cannot be the defining criterion for protecting species or individuals.

Each year, millions of animals die unnaturally early deaths to satisfy our taste for animal flesh when these same animals possess a rich mental life—a life of far greater emotional and intellectual depth than we care to recognize, and a mental life that sometimes far surpasses that of some human beings. The thin veneer of intellectual superiority can no more justify our eating of animals than it would permit the eating of average humans by some carnivorous, superintelligent extraterrestrial.

In the end, it is consciousness, simple or reflexive, and not intelligence, that is the morally relevant criterion for protecting certain species. It is the possession of consciousness that is the basis for our *prima facie* obligation not to kill a species. Consciousness has intrinsic value. It far transcends even the weighing of pleasure and pain that can occur only because of—only as an object of—the experience of consciousness. Experience of existence—consciousness—has a significance all its own; all other values inhere in and depend upon this more fundamental constant. This explains, as one philosopher has put it, why we would rather spend a day mildly depressed than drugged out of consciousness.[39] It also explains why we should protect animals, infants, and the mentally handicapped. Though their respective intellectual capacities may vary, all are conscious, sentient, experiencing beings in the world. This alone makes their lives sacred.

Just as consciousness has intrinsic value, so too, the development and complexity of consciousness may be the basis for ascribing to certain species an interest over and above certain other species in limited circumstances. But this moral advantage, as it were, does not amount to anything near absolute dominion. Rather, it gives the more advanced species an interest only to the extent that its sheer survival depends upon a not-too-burdensome sacrifice on the part of the less-developed species. The life of a conscious being may never be taken except to safeguard the survival of a more-developed being; convenience and convention are never enough to justify killing another sentient being. And even here the burden placed upon the less developed species must not be too great. This explains why humans should not consume animals, and why the captain of the sinking ship was right to sacrifice the dog before one of his human passengers.

In this chapter, I have argued that the case for vegetarianism can be made out either on utilitarian or deontological grounds. As I argued in chapter 1, however, deontological considerations of rights should take precedence over the utilitarian weighing of interests. This is true for both psychological and moral reasons. As a psychological matter, the experience of pleasure and pain, which is of fundamental importance to the utilitarian, is itself dependent upon the more fundamental capacity for consciousness, sentience or subjective experience, the basis for our argument here. Morally, as we saw in chapter 1, the problem of trading on the rights of some to advance the interests of others—the problem of justice—is unjustifiable. Thus, there is a place for utilitarian theory but it is a subordinate place in our moral analysis. The utilitarian weighing of pleasures and pains may take place within and between species only after we have observed this more fundamental deontological principle that might be dubbed the "sanctity of sentience."

Chapter Three

The Argument from
Personal Health

On virtually any moral theory, from the happiness-maximizing utilitarian to the duty-devoted deontologist, and from the Aristotelian pursuer of virtue to the self-seeking ethical egoist, any practice that promises to promote human health is a good thing. The premise is almost so obvious as not to warrant explicit mention. If a certain form of diet were optimal in bettering health and in preventing or eliminating some of the hazards endemic of other dietary habits and practices, such a diet would have to be recommended as part of the achievement of the good life.

As we have seen, many philosophers have extolled the virtues of a vegetarian diet, both for its benefits to health and for its other advantages. In Plato's *Republic*, for example, Socrates prescribes vegetarianism as the diet for his ideal society.[1]

In the modern era, John Wesley, the founder of the Methodist church, extolled the virtues of vegetarianism in this way: "Thanks be to Good: since I gave up flesh and wine, I have been delivered from all physical ills."[2] Others have recognized the psychological, even spiritual, benefits of vegetarianism. Albert Einstein said, "It is my view that the vegetarian manner of living, by its purely physical effect on the human temperament, would most beneficially influence the lot of mankind."[3]

What has been known and reported anecdotally for thousands of years is now scientifically verifiable. In the course of the past century, and particularly in the last two decades, advances in medical science have confirmed and explained the benefits to health in the vegetarian diet. From the standpoint of health, the superiority of the vegetarian diet is no longer in question, even among some of the most conservative members of the medical profession.

Before turning to these issues, however, we first must take a detour in considering the question: Are human beings natural meat eaters? If we could get free of the bonds of culture, would we be omnivores or would we maintain a herbivorous diet? And what relevance does this have for the case for vegetarianism?

Herbivores, Omnivores, and
the Natural-Law Argument

What are humans "meant" to eat? This is a question that routinely arises in the context of the debate over vegetarianism. Is meat eating our "natural" diet? What does "natural" mean exactly, anyway? Moreover, does the fact that a particular diet may be natural, by some definition, mean that alternatives are somehow improper—inappropriate in some physiological, if not moral, sense? As we shall see, defenders of an omnivorous diet have often turned to natural-law arguments in justifying their respective claims to intellectual legitimacy. (For their part, vegetarians have occasionally been guilty of the same.)[4]

Down through the history of Western thought, various forms of natural-law argument have been employed in defense of a wide variety of social and religious practices, customs, requirements, or taboos. From the Roman Catholic proscription against contraception and abortion to the injunction barring homosexuality, and from such noble causes as the demand for universal human rights to such repressive measures as the subjugation of women, natural rights and natural law argument have often found themselves at the center of social issues and ideologies. They have more recently crept into the debate over the proper form of human diet.

As the term implies, the natural-law argument moves from a premise concerning the naturalness or unnaturalness of some particular act or practice to a conclusion that holds that this same practice is morally required or morally intolerable. What is meant by "natural," however, is a matter of some controversy. In a philosophical context, the natural may be that which occurs spontaneously, a result of the laws of nature or the imperatives of each thing's drive for self-realization. In the theological context, the natural is simply that which conforms to the will of God and that occurs in accordance with God's worldly laws.

In the modern usage of the term "natural law," to the extent that it survives explicitly today, it often means "that which occurs in nature." With this modern usage, the natural is sometimes simply held to be that which takes place with some statistical regularity. Of course, many things that are natural by this latter definition may be quite unnatural by some of the others; for example, deviant sexual practices, head-hunting, and polygamy may be statistically frequent in certain cultural contexts and yet remain quite unnatural in more traditional accounts. Conversely, many things that are all too infrequent may be more natural in the sense that they conduce to a better life. Thus, peace among nations, the equitable distribution of wealth, or personal virtue may be unnatural in the sense that they are rare, and yet they may be far more natural in the sense that they are necessary conditions to human happiness.

In the Western tradition, the earliest systematic exponent of what we would today call natural-law argument was Aristotle. Writing in the fourth century B.C., Aristotle maintained that each thing in the universe has a natural *telos*—a purpose, end, or goal toward which it strives and that represents that thing's greatest potential. (See chapter 1) Accordingly, a particular practice or habit was natural if it assisted in the achievement of a thing's *telos*, and unnatural if it prevented reaching this natural end.

Stoic philosophers, who began to flourish shortly after the time of Aristotle's death in 323 B.C. and came to wide popularity two centuries later, also incorporated a form of natural-law thinking into their philosophy. The Stoics believed that the universe was governed by a lawlike, harmonious order, which they called *logos*. The *logos* was an impersonal force that was viewed to regulate the growth, movement, and disintegration of all things in the universe. The Stoics taught that, by acting in conformity with the *logos*, people would be acting according to the natural order of things. A life in conformity with nature meant a life of quiet equanimity and restraint, an existence grounded not in willful resistance to nature, but rather, in "going with the flow" of life. (As such, there are certain interesting parallels between Stoic and eastern Taoist thought.)

Natural-law theory found its way into Christian thinking at two points in church history. Initially, Roman Stoicism influenced early Christianity in the first few centuries after Christ. The Christians replaced the impersonal *logos* of the Stoics with the personal deity, but the notion of a natural or rational order in the universe, presided over by God, was retained. Stoic influences are widely evident in the writings of St. Augustine (354-430), the first true Christian philosopher, and in the thought of the early church fathers.

Almost a thousand years later, in the thirteenth century, a second exponent of natural-law theory influenced Christian (Roman Catholic) theology; this was St. Thomas Aquinas. Aquinas had read Aristotle, whose writings had been lost to the West for over a thousand years until they were rediscovered through recent contacts with the Arab world. Aquinas was responsible for formulating a powerful blend of Aristotelian and Christian thought that has influenced Christian, particularly Roman Catholic, theology ever since.

Through these various influences, Christian natural-law argument held that certain behaviors were unhealthful, both in a worldly and in an otherworldly sense. As men and women were God's creation, God forbade that which was physically and spiritually harmful to humans. Thus, all forms of behavior that were subversive to health or spirit were deemed unnatural and, with an additional logical assumption, morally impermissible.

As we saw in chapter 2, even if the early Christians had embraced vegetarianism as an essential tenet of the faith, this belief was subsequently abandoned; indeed, vegetarianism was even outlawed by the time of Constantine. Thus, the later church philosophers, with the exception of a few heterodox thinkers who argued for the moral necessity of vegetarianism, never took a position on the naturalness of meat eating, one way or the other. In short, during the period when natural law was at its zenith in influence, the question of the naturalness of meat eating was seldom, if ever, raised.

It was later, however, with the enlightenment and the rise of science, that the long tradition of natural-law theory took on a secularized form. It was here that the lingering vestiges of natural law, combined with recent medical and anthropological evidence, assumed the guise of authoritative arguments for, and occasionally against, the propriety of meat eating.

These modern "naturalized" versions of the natural-law argument look to the laws of biology and the principles of human physiology, along with recent anthropological discoveries, in claiming that the human body is constructed in such a way so as to make one form of diet superior to another. What makes one diet more "natural" than another, by this account, is not that it is in conformity with God's will or the dictates of an impersonal universal *logos*, but whether it conforms with our physiological and anatomical structure or, alternatively, was statistically more frequent as an historical or anthropological matter, than another form of diet.

To the chagrin of vegetarian defenders of the modern form of the natural-law argument, modern anthropological discoveries have established that our evolutionary precursors were undoubtedly omnivores. While at least one earlier theory held that our species did not turn to omnivorism until the Ice Age, when shortages of plant food compelled our distant ancestors to kill other animals to survive, more recent evidence has firmly refuted this view.[5] Today, the flesh of other animals, often smaller monkeys, probably accounts for between 1 and 5 percent of the diet of our more distant relatives, chimpanzees and baboons.[6] In the case of our first hominoid ancestors, some evidence indicates that only *Australopithecus robustus* was a vegetarian; the other hominoidal precursors of *Homo sapiens*, *Australopithecus africanus*, *Homo habilis* and *Homo erectus*, were all scavengers and hunters.[7]

By two million years ago, meat comprised roughly 30 percent of the diet of our precursors, usually from small animals or the young of larger animals.[8] Meat represents a similar portion of the diet of precivilized peoples today; about a quarter of the diet of aboriginal peoples and the South African Kung-San consists of meat.[9] By a million years ago, large hunting expeditions were targeting big game.[10] If the "natural" diet is that of our evolutionary forbears, then the vegetarian is obliged to admit that omnivorism, rather than vegetarianism, is natural. (Of course, the current diet of most Americans and others in the First World would still be "unnaturally" high in meat by this standard.) At

any rate, the evidence from the anthropological record is no great
support for the case for vegetarianism.

The anatomical and physiological evidence, however, generally goes the other way. When an overall comparison of the human body is made with those of both carnivores and herbivores,
human anatomy is clearly closer to that of the herbivore. This is
evident particularly in the digestive systems of herbivorous animals. First, carnivores, tend to have long teeth and claws, while
herbivorous animals have no need for these attributes. Herbivores
sweat through their skin, as humans do, while carnivores regulate body heat by rapid breathing and the outward extension of
the tongue. Humans also share the characteristic of most herbivores in possessing a compound known as ptyalin in the saliva.
This compound permits the predigestion of starches, necessary
for the consumption of plant foods; carnivores, on the other hand,
lack ptyalin.

Conversely, carnivores secrete large quantities of hydrochlo-
ric acid (HCL), which is necessary to dissolve bones, teeth, and
other nonfleshy portions of their prey. Humans secrete little HCL,
as do most herbivorous animals. Further, from an anatomical
standpoint, the jaws of carnivores typically move only vertical-
ly, while those of humans and herbivores move sideways as well.
Carnivores also generally lap liquids with the tongue, while herbivores suck liquid through the teeth, as can humans.[11]

Finally, and perhaps most significantly, humans possess the
long intestines of herbivores. Carnivores tend to have very short
bowels, a biological necessity given the fact that animal flesh
rots and toxifies much more quickly than does plant food.
The carnivore must process its meal quickly in order to avoid
the toxic effects inherent in the decomposition of meat. On
the other hand, herbivores may process the food longer, deriv-
ing more nutritional benefit as a result of the longer digestive
period.[12]

What does this evidence, taken together, suggest as to the
question of human diet? Probably less than modern defenders of
vegetariansim and omnivorism would prefer. The equivocal implications of the anthropological, anatomical, and physiological
data may be the result of the fact that, throughout the course of
the past two million years or so, we have eaten omnivorously.

Consequently, we may possess both herbivorous and carnivorous characteristics. But even if the scientific evidence was univocal, one way or the other, it would have little significance in a moral sense.

Natural-law arguments and their ilk have long been criticized by philosophers on two grounds: First, as we have just observed in this discussion, there exists great controversy as to what we mean by "natural" in the first place. In the most general sense, everything that takes place is natural in the sense that there are (natural) scientific laws that explain each thing's occurrence. By this definition, both vegetarianism and omnivorism would be natural in the sense that humans have observed both forms of diet. But if something like this definition guides our use of the term, the second problem arises—namely, it does not follow from the fact that some practice is "natural" that it is good or morally preferable to any other practice. War, famine, slavery, exploitation, and every other worldly ill are all natural in the sense that they occur with some regularity in the world. However, they are not natural in the sense that we wish to promote or emulate these practices.

Another way to view this difficulty can be expressed by recourse to what has been dubbed "the naturalistic fallacy." The naturalistic fallacy arises when moving from a factual premise about the "naturalness" of a particular practice to a moral conclusion about its rightness or wrongness. In the cant of popular philosophy, one cannot go from an "is" to an "ought"—from a fact about the naturalness (e.g., the statistical frequency) of a particular practice or act such as eating meat, to a conclusion concerning its moral propriety.

In sum, where the tern "natural" is reduced, as it is in the modern sense, to that which exists as a factual matter, it takes on a purely descriptive quality, losing all its *prescriptive* significance. It does not purport to tell us how we *ought* to behave, but simply how we *have behaved* in the past, hardly a standard by which to measure our future aspirations, morally, socially and otherwise. It is only if another meaning can be assigned to the term "natural," one that still carries with it some normative or moral import, that the natural-law argument may have something to say about how we ought to act.

"If God Had Not Meant for Man to Eat Meat . . ." The Natural-Law Argument Reconsidered

Claims to the naturalness of meat eating are placed in question by the ambiguity of the scientific evidence: while the diet of our precursors consisted of meat, much of our anatomical and physiological apparatus appears to be geared to a herbivorous diet. More significantly, neither our species' history nor our biology is necessarily our destiny. The fact that the diet of our ancestors may have consisted partially of meat is no particular indication that this is the best, the most natural, or the healthiest, form of diet. Our ancestors engaged in many forms of behavior, from head-hunting to the eating of rocks and dirt, which have been happily relinquished along the way to civilization. Historical precedent was no more a reason for refusing to abandon these practices than it is a justification for eating meat.

Nearly a century ago, detractors of the airplane mused, in natural-law fashion, "If God had meant for us to fly, He would have given us wings." Today, the meat eater might be heard to echo a similar refrain: "If God had not meant for us to eat meat, He wouldn't have given us animals and the brains to catch them with." But it does not follow that we *should* do something—that it is right or most healthful—because we *have* done it or because we *can* do it. This defense of meat eating is no more persuasive than were similar admonitions concerning recent scientific innovations at the beginning of this century.

On the other hand, there is one sense of the word "natural" that may permit a conclusion to be drawn about the superiority of the vegetarian diet. If one diet is more healthful than another—if it better serves our species in terms of fostering longer lives with fewer maladies and promoting our daily vitality and sense of well-being, then this diet has a strong claim to being the most natural. In short, the genuine mark of the natural is not that which is most statistically frequent, either currently or as a historical matter, but that which optimally serves the function of the human organism. In a very real sense, we are back to Aristotle: the most natural diet is the one that best serves our *telos*, that promotes health and longevity and that permits us to pursue our respective visions of the good life.

But what evidence is there for the claim that vegetarianism is the more healthful diet? What makes one form of diet more "healthful" in the first place?

A Holistic Concept of Health

In the ever-expanding realm to which science and technology have laid claim, the terms "sickness" and "health" have attained increasingly broad interpretations. Once a measurement only of physical well-being, the concept of health now is generally recognized to embrace the mental realm, as in the notion of mental health, the spiritual realm, and even the social and political domains, as when we speak of crime as a "social sickness." This expanded scope of the concept of health was recognized and enshrined by the World Health Organization in 1946 when it declared that: "Health is a state of complete physical, mental and social well-being and not merely the absence of disease or infirmity."[13]

In the remainder of this chapter, we will examine the benefits of the vegetarian diet to physical health, but our investigation will not be limited to this. Even if one chooses not to go as far as the World Health Organization in extending the concept of health to a range of political and social ills, it is similarly clear that it cannot be limited to the physical realm. We now have strong evidence not only that physical health is necessary to mental well-being, but that poor mental health may have a range of debilitating effects upon the physical organism. In short, mental and physical health are intimately intertwined, mutually dependent and reciprocally interactive. A holistic conception of health is a way of transcending the dualisms of the past—the dichotomies of mind and body, self and world, prevention and cure. By making it clear that health, in its fullest sense, is a function of both our physical bodies and our mental perspective—our sense of zest for life, the meaning we derive from our existence, the potentiality of our experience—we learn to recognize the interdependence of body and mind.

Similarly, by recognizing that we are affected by the way we live in the world—that there are discernible psychological consequences to ourselves that result from the way we view ourselves as we interact with others—we come to understand that our state of health, most broadly defined, is *not* simply a function of *what we do to ourselves*. As we interact with the world, we give ourselves cues. Psychologically, we cannot expect the world to be any kinder to us than we are to it. Consequently, the way in which we interact with the world reverberates in our psyches and in our self-conceptions. We are psychologically, as well as physically, bound to the world. We cannot—and generally do not—expect healthy selves in an unhealthy world. Nor do we expect to find the healthy psyche engaged in acts of unmitigated selfishness or outright brutality. We cannot help but place ourselves, albeit temporarily, in the shoes of the Other whom we victimize or neglect. The doctrine of karma has potent psychological, if not cosmic, significance to our own continued well-being.

Finally, by recognizing that health is a function of the way we live our lives at all times and is not just a matter of what we do when we are ill, we will come to understand that good health is not a product of good cures. It is the cumulative result of good living.

The argument from health is compelling enough when we look to the physical benefits of vegetarianism, as well as to the disastrous consequences of meat eating. When we also consider the psychological and even the spiritual effects of vegetarianism, we will see that the argument from health can be made in the strongest possible terms.

The Varieties and Benefits
of the Vegetarian Diet

Vegetarianism is not a univocal concept; it embraces a wide range of dietary options all of which have only one thing in common: each and all exclude the consumption of meat. Within this range, however, the form of vegetarian diet one adopts may have much to do with one's reasons for becoming a vegetarian in the first place. For example, the range of options spans from the less restrictive lacto-ovo vegetarianism, a diet that permits eggs and dairy products along with all other fruits and vegetables—in essence, everything but meat products is permitted—to those adhering to a strict macrobiotic diet and who may eat only brown rice. Between these two poles are those who abstain from egg products, but may continue to consume dairy products (lacto vegetarians), those who eat egg products but abstain from dairy products (ovo vegetarians), those who will eat no animal products whatsoever (vegans), less-strict adherents of the macrobiotic diet (who eat whole grains, legumes, vegetables, and miso, but who do not eat fruit), natural hygienists (who eat only unprocessed or unrefined plant foods), "raw foodists" (who eat only uncooked and unprocessed plant foods) and fruitarians (who will eat only nuts, fruits, and vegetable-fruits, such as tomatoes and peppers).

Here, use of the term "vegetarian" to apply to those who eat fish and fowl, but not red meat, is eschewed. This popular use of the term, though disconcertingly widespread, is a gross misnomer. Though even lacto-ovo vegetarians include some non-vegetable products in their diet, and so might be thought not to be true vegetarians, at least they do not eat meat. In this respect, the term "vegetarian" has some general descriptive appeal, even if not strictly accurate. On the other hand, how anyone could think that a chicken is not meat truly remains one of the great intellectual curiosities of our time.

A recent survey indicates that 34 percent of all vegetarians in the United States are lacto-ovo vegetarians, 3 percent are ovo vegetarians, 11 percent are lacto vegetarians, while the largest single group are vegans, who make up about 39 percent of the vegetarian population. The remaining 13 percent surveyed fell into one of the other dietary classifications, including raw foodists, natural hygienists, adherents to the macrobiotic diet, and others. The median age for vegetarians surveyed was thirty five years old. The median length of time that those from this group had been vegetarian was eight years.[14] Thus, vegetarianism is no fad for most who embrace this dietary alternative.

While the verdict is still out on some of the more extreme forms of vegetarianism such as certain forms of the macrobiotic diet, it is now clear that vegans and lacto-ovo vegetarians have no problem in achieving the necessary dietary intake on a daily basis. For the lacto-ovo (or pure lacto or ovo) vegetarian, dietary adequacy has never been seriously questioned. Even if a diet of pure vegetable sources had been found to be nutritionally deficient, the addition of eggs or dairy products to a well-balanced diet guarantees the lacto-ovo vegetarian the protein and vitamins thought by some to be lacking in a vegan diet. Moreover, the ease with which one can assume the lacto-ovo vegetarian diet or one of its variations, both from a nutritional and a social standpoint, make it a likely first step for many vegetarians. Indeed, on anything vaguely approaching a balanced diet, the lacto-ovo vegetarian has nothing to fear concerning the nutritional adequacy of her diet.[15]

It is with the vegan diet that some nutritionists once drew the line. The fear was that a diet of purely vegetable sources would be insufficient in protein, iron, and a few important vitamins, particularly vitamins B/12 and D. As we shall see in a subsequent section, the protein scare was the result of a card overplayed by the meat and dairy industries with the help of their government lobbyists. Americans now consume roughly two-and-a-half times as much protein as is nutritionally necessary.[16] Even vegans can easily achieve more than the recommended daily allowance in protein from a diet free of all animal products. (See the section, "Of Protein and Propaganda," in this chapter.) Moreover, an overabundance of protein has been linked to a range of health problems, including osteoporosis, kidney disease, and certain forms of cancer, which typically affect older persons in America and other wealthy nations today. The well-balanced vegan diet is more than nutritionally adequate in terms of protein and also avoids the hazards of excessive protein intake characteristic of the diet in wealthier nations today. Another nutritional fallacy holds that the vegetarian diet is deficient in iron. Some may fear that they run the risk of becoming anemic if they relinquish meat eating. In fact, studies indicate that the hemoglobin levels of vegetarians (both vegan and lacto-ovo vegetarians) are consistently higher than that of meat-eaters.[17] A variety of vegetable sources are rich in iron, including green leafy vegetables (particularly spinach), certain dried fruits (especially raisins, dried tomatoes and prunes), and a range of other vegetable products.

Loss of iron is a significant problem for menstruating women. Meat-eating women, however, possess thicker uterine tissues and higher levels of estrogen in the blood. Thicker tissues in the uterine wall lead to heavier menstrual bleeding with a resultant greater loss of iron. Higher levels of estrogen are associated with longer and heavier menstrual periods. For both reasons, not only can vegetarian women achieve sufficient intake of iron, they appear to *retain* iron better.[18]

Nor need the vegan worry about a deficit in the amount of vitamin B/12 or D, as once concerned some dietary specialists. While neither of these vitamin nutrients is found in fresh plant foods, the vegetarian diet poses no obstacle to nutritional adequacy in these areas. First, vitamin D is produced by the human body. A short walk in the sunlight enables the human body to synthesize more than enough vitamin D to meet its daily nutritional requirements. (For lighter skinned individuals, ten minutes in the sun is sufficient; for dark-skinned, as much as forty minutes may be necessary.)[19] In addition, fortified milk has plenty of D for the lacto-ovo vegetarian; soy milk similarly provides enough for the vegan. Thus, the lacto-ovo vegetarian easily consumes more D than is nutritionally necessary while even those who abstain from all animal products can assure themselves of sufficient dietary vitamin D.

As for vitamin B/12, only a very tiny amount is nutritionally necessary. Again, getting enough B/12 is no problem whatsoever for the lacto-ovo vegetarian, who consumes more than enough each day by eating egg and dairy products. As for the vegan, B/12 is available through the eating of tempeh (a fermented soy product that has become popular in "tempeh burgers.") A small amount of B/12 is also produced by the microflora in the human body. This may explain why vegans with well-balanced diets show no B/12 deficiencies.[20] Finally, vitamin supplements are always there for the wary. Indeed, John Robbins, the heir to the Baskin-Robbins ice cream empire who argues for an end to meat and dairy product consumption, recommends that strict vegans take B/12 supplements.[21]

In sum, lacto-ovo vegetarians have nothing to fear in the way of dietary insufficiency as long as they maintain anything remotely approaching a balanced diet. The lacto-ovo vegetarian is on roughly the same nutritional ground as the meat eater. While the vegan must be more careful to maintain a balanced diet, the vegan can obtain all her nutrients from plant sources. To be certain, however, the vegan can assure dietary adequacy with vitamin supplements.

What do vegetarians themselves say about the health benefits of the vegetarian option? In a recent survey, 84 percent of all vegetarians surveyed reported an improvement in physical health. Nine percent reported no change. (Of the 7 percent who reported a worsening of health, half said their problems were short-term difficulties in making the dietary transition. As for the remaining 3 to 4 percent, we cannot be certain whether difficulties were related to an an inadequate diet or to other health problems that may have resulted independent of the change of diet.)[22]

The specific benefits of vegetarianism were reported to be many and varied. Thirty-one percent reported an increase in energy or stamina, 21 percent said they were ill less often, 16 percent reported the amelioration or cure of a pre-existing health problem, 10 percent reported improved regularity, 8 percent noted better complexion, hair, nails, and such, while 7 percent claimed the transition to vegetarianism helped bring a weight problem under control.[23] Over a quarter of those surveyed reported a general improvement in physical and mental well-being. Others experienced still other interesting changes, including an enhanced ability to give up various bad habits, particularly smoking and alcohol.[24]

Meat Eating and the Diseases of Affluence

The transition to vegetarianism is beneficial to health in two general and distinct ways. The consumption of more fruit and vegetable matter is affirmatively health producing in providing more fiber, vitamins and nutrients to the human diet. But the vegetarian diet is at least as significant for what it does *not* have—for the elimination of the *negative* aspects of meat eating.

The salutary effects of vegetarianism can be seen by looking to a number of situations, historically and cross-culturally, where, for cultural, geographic, political, or economic reasons, reliance on animal products was reduced or eliminated. One of the most interesting of such instances occurred in Denmark during World War I. Between October of 1917 and October of 1918, a British blockade of Denmark prevented the importation of meat. The Danes were forced to live on a diet of milk, vegetables, and grains during this period. During this same period, the death rate dropped dramatically—by 34 percent. The correlation between the blockade and the death rate is highlighted by the fact that there were far fewer deaths during this period than there were for any similar period over the course of the previous eighteen years. Moreover, once the blockade was lifted and people returned to their previous diet of meat, the death rate returned to its usual level. A government medical official attributed the markedly reduced death rate during the period of the blockade to the change in diet.[25] While it may remain a question as to how the death rate responded so quickly to the forced dietary transition, and again to the reversion to a meat-eating diet, the dramatic change in rate along with the concurrence of this change with the change in diet makes it difficult not to see a connection between the two.

A similar correlation between life expectancy and diet can be observed by looking at cultures with radically distinct diets. Again, the correlation between meat eating and a lowered life expectancy is striking, all the more so when one considers that some with the longest lifespans often live in conditions of severe poverty. The Russian Caucasians, the Yucatan Indians, the East Indian Todas, and the Pakistani Hunzakuts live on diets with little or no animal products. All of these groups have average lifespans of ninety to one hundred years. Imagine how long those in more affluent, cleaner, and more medically advanced countries might live if they were to relinquish meat eating. Conversely, populations with the highest rates of meat in the diet—Eskimos, Laplanders, Greenlanders, and the Russian Kurgi tribes—also have the lowest life expectancies, which average little more than thirty years.[26] The obvious correlation can even be witnessed in the context of the same culture over the course of only two generations: in Japan, over the course of the past four decades, increased wealth has brought higher rates of meat eating and, with it, much higher rates of heart disease, cancer and diabetes than at any previous time in the nation's history.

The diseases of affluence—heart disease, cancer, and diabetes—so called because their incidence is much higher in wealthy nations where diets are rich in meat, sugar, and refined foods, are the conditions that top the list as killers in the United States and other parts of the First World. Heart disease and cancer are the first and second most significant causes of death in the United States today, respectively. Both are inextricably linked to meat-eating. Heart disease is most generally precipitated by three factors: high cholesterol, high blood pressure and smoking.[27] The first two of these three variables are directly and positively affected by a reduction in meat eating. Plant food contains much lower levels of saturated fats and no cholesterol. Cholesterol and fat have, in turn, been linked with high blood pressure. In sum, by reducing cholesterol and fat from the diet, one can substantially reduce one's chances of heart disease. Elimination of meat from the diet is the most effective way of doing this.

As might be expected from what has already been said, lacto-ovo vegetarians have a greatly reduced risk of heart disease (one-third that of meat eaters), while the risk is cut even more radically with a vegan diet (to one-tenth that of meat eaters).[28] Further, the medical consensus on the link between diet and heart disease is now virtually unanimous; in a recent survey, 99 percent of scientists and medical researchers actively involved with arteriosclerotic problems affirmed the connection between fat and cholesterol, on the one hand, and heart disease, on the other.[29] Many doctors now recommend the reduction or elimination of meat from the diet as the *best* way to prevent heart disease.

Excessive levels of fat in the diet play a role not only in heart disease but in various forms of cancer.[30] According to the Centers for Disease Control, thirty four million Americans are at least moderately overweight.[31] This is largely the result of our nation's overconsumption of meat. As one typical example, to consume 23 grams of protein (an amount that represents over half the daily protein required for a woman of average size and about 40 percent of what the average man requires, according to the U.S. Department of Agriculture) from a serving of lean meat, one must also consume 350 grams of fat, an amount well in excess of the recommended daily amount of fat for men and women.[32] In essence, meat eating is an extremely inefficient—and outright dangerous—way to get your protein.

Moreover, not only are we getting too much fat, we are getting the wrong kind of fat. Saturated fats pose the greatest health risk of all. The link between red meat, high in saturated fats, and colon cancer is now well established; those who eat red meat every day are two-and-a-half times as likely to develop colon cancer as those who eat it sparingly. Moreover, colon cancer is ten times as frequent in the United States and other beef-eating cultures as compared to vegetarian or semivegetarian Asian cultures.[33] Again, as the evidence with Japan indicates, the relevant factor in the incidence of disease appears to be nutritional, rather than genetic or cultural: it is our diets, and not our genetic endowment, which is responsible for this problem. Similarly, research comparing the national average of fat consumption in countries around the world with national rates of breast cancer indicate an almost one-to-one linear correspondence between the two, strongly suggesting a causal relationship between the meat consumption and cancer.[34]

The link between meat eating and various forms of cancer has been borne out in a variety of ways. One early study focused on Seventh Day Adventists, whose religion prescribes a vegetarian diet. It found that the incidence of cancers of the lung, mouth, larynx, and esophagus were only one-eighth what the researchers expected them to be by comparison with the general population.[35] Of course, Adventists not only refrain from meat, they also abstain from alcohol and tobacco; thus, the lowered rate of cancer may be the result of the generally healthful lifestyle of members of this group. Nevertheless, a difference by a factor of eight should be encouraging news to the vegetarian, particularly since, on average, vegetarians similarly have a marked lower incidence of smoking and alcohol consumption.

More recent studies have confirmed the relationship between cancer and diet. John Robbins quotes a recent article in the journal *Advances in Cancer Research* that concludes, "At present, we have overwhelming evidence . . . (that) none of the risk factors for cancer is . . . more significant than diet and nutrition."[36] In the last decade or two, researchers have discovered a number of reasons for this link. In addition to the causal connection between fat and cancer, recent studies have uncovered two other factors that predispose the meat eater to a higher probability of various forms of cancer. First, the lower the amount of fiber in the diet, the more likely it is that one will develop cancer, particularly cancers of the gastrointestinal tract. Fruits and vegetables are high in fiber. Meat has absolutely no fiber whatsoever.

Yet fiber is needed to ameliorate the effects of the *other* factor that predisposes meat eaters to cancer—toxins in the meat. These toxins are the residue of antibiotics, growth hormones, and other dangerous chemicals used in modern meat production. (See the following section.) Fiber is instrumental in absorbing these toxins, which are released from meat in the process of digestion. Ironically, the more meat one eats, the greater the amount of carcinogenic toxins released in the digestive process, which, at the same time, makes it considerably less likely the meat eater will consume the amount of fiber necessary to absorb these carcinogenic toxins.

Every year, heart disease takes a million lives in the United States alone. Cancer kills over half a million others. While people continue to die, and while the government and private citizens spend billions of dollars supporting the search for a cure for these diseases of affluence, we overlook the most viable solution of all: prevention. A change in diet, preferably to a completely meat-free dietary regimen, poses by far the easiest, most cost-efficient, and best response to the diseases of affluence.

Look What's Coming with Dinner: Meat Toxicity

Yet another hazard of meat is the result of what is *in* it when the consumer purchases and eats it. In this section, we will consider two kinds of meat toxicity: that which is caused by chemicals used in the course of meat production and a variety of diseases that are passed on to the consumer through meat.

One of the most distressing aspects of modern meat production, driven by the profit motive and facilitated by mass production techniques rivaled only by the automotive industry, is the use, overuse, and abuse of a plethora of chemicals used in the course of raising chickens, cows, pigs, and other farm animals. Today, meat is systematically shot up with growth hormones, antibiotics, antitoxins (which are themselves toxic), pesticides, and vermicides. These chemicals do not magically disappear when the carcass that was once an animal is sold to the consumer. They remain in the meat and are consumed by those who eat it. Most of these chemicals are carcinogens. Many adversely affect the human auto-immune system.[37]

The Food and Drug Administration reported not long ago that as many as five hundred to six hundred distinct chemicals may be present in the nation's meat supply. Yet no adequate program to monitor and test meat for these substances exists. More specifically, the Office of Technology Assessment has found that "nearly all poultry, most pigs and veal calves and 60 percent of cattle get antibiotic additives." Moreover, 75 percent of pigs eat feed laced with sulfa drugs.[38] Fourteen percent of meat and poultry products randomly tested by the Department of Agriculture contained illegally high levels of pesticides and drugs. A report issued by the department stated that at least forty-two of these substances are known to cause cancer or are suspected of causing cancer, twenty are known to cause birth defects and six cause mutations.[39] This number is undoubtedly optimistically low. Since this report was issued, the number and rate of use of these chemicals has only risen. Moreover, still others of these chemicals have since been discovered to cause cancer, autoimmune disorders, and a variety of other dangerous conditions in humans.

The level of use of these chemicals can be seen from the standpoint of the sales figures of manufacturers of antibiotics, pesticides, and other chemicals. Half of all antibiotics sold in the United States are fed to cattle, chickens, and other animals.[40] Eighty percent of all herbicides used in the United States are sprayed on corn and soybeans, much of which is then fed to livestock. According to the National Research Council of the National Academy of Sciences, beef pesticide contamination represents 11 percent of the total cancer risk to consumers from all foods on the market—and this does not include the cancer risk from the meat itself.[41]

The indirect ingestion of antibiotics poses a double-edged threat to human health, independent of the risk of cancer. First, the regular consumption of antibiotics is related to a weakened response on the part of the human immune system. This may leave the individual increasingly susceptible to a variety of illnesses and conditions ranging from pneumonia to certain forms of cancer.[42] Second, the high concentration of antibiotics in meat have led to a variety of strains of supermicroorganisms—

antibiotic-resistant bacteria that cause such illnesses and conditions as diarrhea, septicaemia, psittacosis, salmonella, gonorrhea,
pneumonia, typhoid, and childhood meningitis.[43] Thus, not only
may the various organisms that carry these diseases be present
in meat, they may be untreatable by the antibiotics typically utilized to combat them.

The use of pesticides and other dangerous chemicals in meat
production is particularly alarming because of the high concentrations in which they are found in meat. Fruits and vegetables
also contain toxic chemicals, particularly pesticides, and vermicides, but the concentrations of these chemicals is much less significant lower on the food chain. Animals, on the other hand,
eat large quantities of plant food and store a correspondingly
higher amount of the chemical residue contained in the vegetable matter.[44] These dangerously high concentrations of chemicals
are, of course, consumed by humans when meat is eaten.

In addition to the range of chemicals used in the raising of
animals for meat, consumers now also must be wary of what
else goes into the food of their food. In an effort to hold down
the costs of feed, feedlots have begun to experiment with a variety of artificial substances designed to add weight and bulk to
livestock but that provide no nutritional benefit to animals. Researcher Jeremy Rifkin reports that feedlots now sometimes add
cardboard, newspaper, and sawdust into animal feed. In some
cases, chicken manure is added directly to cattle feed. Some have
predicted that cement dust may become big in the future; it produces weight gain 30 percent faster than regular feed. Researchers are even experimenting with plastic pellets, one advantage
of which would be that a cow's rumen could be melted down
and recycled as part of the feed for the next generation.[45]

Of course, these fillers fulfill no more nutritional requirements
for the human consumers of meat than they did for the animals
who had them first. In most cases, this means no nutritional
advantage at all, and an overall decline in the nutritional value
of the meat. Moreover, we cannot yet adequately gauge the range
of negative effects of these fillers on the health of human consumers. Needless to say, the chemical and biological residue of
newspaper, cardboard, plastic, and chicken manure is no more
nutritionally promising than it is appetizing.

Consumers of meat also face a wholly distinct set of problems in terms of the transmission of a number of diseases from animals to humans. Again, when humans incorporate the flesh of animals into their own systems, they often get more than they bargain for. The two most common types of diseases to affect farm animals for our purposes here are salmonella and various forms of cancer. The connection between the infected animal and human illness is well established in the case of salmonella; only recently, however, have scientists begun to suspect that there is a similar connection between animal meat and human cancer.

Chicken products routinely carry salmonella. An estimated one-third to one-half of all chicken meat marketed in the United States in contaminated with salmonellosis. The dramatic rise of salmonella in the 1980s was the result of intensified chicken-farming practices characterized by stuffing as many chickens as possible into as little cage space as possible and stacking these cages one atop the next in warehouse fashion. Feces from chickens routinely seep through tiny cracks in egg shells and contaminate egg products. Further, in some chicken farms, the disease easily spreads from chicken to chicken as a result of the cramped quarters. In 1988, the Centers for Disease Control announced that Grade A eggs were responsible for an "epidemic rise" in salmonella infection in the northeastern United States. Several people died as a result of salmonella poisoning in this epidemic alone.[46]

Chickens also carry a variety of other dangerous diseases, including certain forms of cancer. A recent government report found that over 90 percent of chickens are afflicted with leukosis, a form of cancer similar to leukemia.[47] The rate of disease among chickens is so high that the Department of Labor has ranked the poultry industry as one of the most hazardous occupations—not for the chickens but for those who raise, slaughter, and process them. If *growing* chickens is this hazardous, what can be said for the wisdom of *eating* them?

The link between animal cancer and human cancer recently has begun to be made by scientists. As we just mentioned, 90 percent of all chickens are carriers of leukosis. Moreover, 20 percent of all cows are afflicted with a variety of cancer known as bovine leukemia virus (BLV). Studies have increasingly linked BLV with HTLV-1, the first human retrovirus discovered to cause

cancer.[48] Perhaps even more frightening, scientists have successfully infected human cells with bovine immunodeficiency virus
(BIV), the equivalent of the AIDS virus in cows. Researchers
believe that BIV may have a role in the development of a number of malignant or slow viruses in humans. Meanwhile, BIV
continues to spread at epidemic rates among cows.[49]

The illnesses and conditions discussed here are merely representative of a whole range of illnesses that affect the various
species of farm animals. It only stands to reason that many, if
not all, of these are transmittable to the human consumers of
meat. And yet, at precisely the time when the meat-inspection
process is most essential to the health of consumers, the wave
of deregulation that swept the federal bureaucracy in the 1980s
has severely minimized the role of the Department of Agriculture in the meat-inspection process. In fact, the effect of recent
deregulation has been to give the job of inspection back to the
meat industry itself. As one federal meat inspector said, "The
whole idea of the meat-packing companies policing themselves
is ridiculous. I've heard the comment that it's like having the
fox guarding the chicken house, and that is exactly the truth."[50]

Of Protein and Propaganda

Perhaps the greatest fear that has dissuaded many would-be vegetarians from choosing a diet free of meat is the claim that the
vegetarian diet does not contain enough protein. So many myths
surround this claim that it might be helpful to survey each of
these, respectively.

Myth Number One: Only animals produce enough protein
to sustain humans in their dietary needs.

This first myth is not only false, it turns the truth completely
on its head. No animal, human or otherwise, produces its own
protein. *Ultimately, all protein comes from plant foods.* Plants
are the only living things that synthesize protein. Indeed, it is
interesting to note that defenders of meat eating have overlooked
the fact that the meat they eat usually comes from animals that
are themselves vegetarian—cows, sheep, pigs, and others. If vegetarian animals get enough protein from their diet, why can't we?

Myth Number Two: While animals are not the original source of protein, they are the best, most efficient, such source.

This myth holds that animal meat contains *more* protein per serving and is, in other respects, a higher quality source of protein in the diet. However, meat does not contain more protein than does plant food. A variety of meatless dishes contain at least as much protein as meat dishes. For example, a peanut butter sandwich on whole wheat bread and a cup of milk contains twenty-two grams of protein—an amount equal to one-half of the forty four grams of protein needed by an adult female daily and about 40 percent of the fifty-six grams required by the average adult male. Similarly, seven ounces of tofu with a cup of cooked brown rice and a small stalk of broccoli contains twenty-five grams of protein. One cup of potatoes contains seven grams of protein, a cup of cooked beans fifteen grams, and a cup of green leafy vegetables five grams. Even a corn muffin has three grams of protein.[51] One almost has to try *not* to get enough protein to fall short on a vegetarian diet.

Another way to view the protein requirement is from the standpoint of percentage of total calories in the diet. While estimates vary, we need somewhere between 2 1/2 to 8 percent of our total dietary calories in the form of protein. Almost any vegetable source has a level of protein well within—and in many cases well above—this required amount. For example, lentils have 29 percent protein by calories, peas 26 percent, cabbage 22 percent, wheat and sunflower seeds 17 percent, oatmeal and pumpkin each 15 percent, and potatoes 11 percent. Thus, a diet complete with a variety of these and similar foods would be high in protein assuming the required amount of calories were consumed.[52]

A corollary of this fact is that the fat-to-protein ratio is much lower in the vegetarian diet. Over 75 percent of all calories in beef, frankfurters, cold cuts and pork are fat. Even "leaner" meats such as chicken, lamb, and veal contain 50 to 75 percent calories by fat.[53] Levels of fat are significantly lower (and sometimes nonexistent) with vegetable sources. Thus, the vegetarian gets an adequate amount of protein with much lower levels of fat consumption (and, as we saw previously, even the type of fat consumed from vegetable products is preferable to the more dangerous animal fat).

The only advantage of meat over plant foods as a source of protein is that meats contain a complete protein; all of the twenty or so amino acids that comprise a complete protein and that are necessary for good health in humans are present in the same meat. Vegetable sources, on the other hand, have to be varied to obtain all of the necessary amino acids. As we shall see next, however, this is so easy to do that meat poses no real advantage at all.

Myth Number Three: If vegetable sources are not carefully balanced in terms of intake of amino acids, such that at every meal a complete protein is consumed, the vegetarian will suffer the effects of protein deficiency.

Enter the world of protein complementarity, a world of carefully measured rations, well-timed meals with specifically chosen dishes meant to adequately "complement" one another in terms of protein adequacy. This was a regimen popularized, if one can call such a prospect "popular," in the first edition of Francis Moore Lappé's *Diet for a Small Planet*.

Lappé began with the assumption that all amino acids have to be consumed roughly simultaneously in order to achieve a "complete protein." She noted that many cultures with largely vegetarian diets had evolved cuisines centering around complementary foods. From corn tortillas and beans in countries south of the border to such combinations as rice and beans, bulgar wheat and garbanzo beans, pita bread and hummus, rice or wheat chapatis with lentil dahl, soy and rice, and soy and barley, among others from other various parts of the world, all combine the essential components of the complete protein. According to the first edition of Lappé's book, these foods, containing these protein elements, had to be combined carefully and in close temporal proximity to ensure that all of the amino acids necessary to the whole protein were consumed.

In the second edition of her book, Lappé reconsidered the assumption from which she started—namely, that consumption of all the amino acids must take place roughly simultaneously—and repudiated the idea. While everyone needs to get all of these fundamental elements, they need not be consumed at once.[54] Indeed, some have gone further, arguing that certain vegetable sources contain enough of all the essential amino acids without resort to complementary sources.[55]

Keep in mind that all of these complimentary concerns are relevant to vegans and others who eschew all animal products, including eggs and milk. Because milk and eggs complete any protein, the lacto-ovo vegetarian has nothing to fear in the way of concerns about protein deficiency.[56] In short, there is no question from even the most traditional meat-and-potatoes viewpoint that the lacto-ovo vegetarian diet is adequate. It is now well accepted, however, that a well-balanced vegan diet is similarly safe.

Myth Number Four: Though it is possible to achieve nutritional adequacy with a vegetarian diet, it is, nonetheless, very difficult. Most vegetarians exhibit a protein deficit.

Nothing could be further from the truth. In fact, while meat eating Americans consume up to two-and-a-half times the amount of protein necessary each day, the U.S. Department of Agriculture—hardly a bastion of radical dietary dogma—has found that vegetarians in this country consumed 150 percent of the required amount of protein each day.[57] The National Research Council of the U.S. National Academy of Sciences, the group responsible for determining the recommended daily allowance of essential vitamins and nutrients, declared as far back as 1974 that the vegetarian diet is nutritionally adequate. Finally, in 1988, the American Dietetic Association reported that, "[v]egetarian diets are healthful and nutritionally adequate when appropriately planned." They added that meat eaters must similarly plan their diets to meet nutritional requirements.[58] Thus, from all quarters, the vegetarian diet has passed muster and been sanctioned as nutritionally sound.

Not only do vegetarians get enough protein, it should also be noted here that increasing evidence points to a number of health problems related to *too much* protein in the diet. The most important of these is the link between excess protein and osteoporosis. Osteoporosis, a condition that affects 25 percent of all women over the age of sixty-five and a smaller number of younger women and men, is characterized by a loss of calcium in the bones causing a brittleness in the bones which renders the sufferer more prone to a variety of injuries, fractures, and breaks in bones.[59]

Studies indicate that a reduction of protein in the diet by 50 percent results in a similar 50 percent reduction in calcium excreted through the kidneys.[60] Apparently, calcium is drawn from the bones in the process of metabolizing excess protein. Where an excess of protein is consumed, normal dietary intake of calcium is not sufficient; extra calcium must be drawn from calcium stores in the bones. This results in osteoporosis. A protein balance of seventy-five grams a day—an amount well in excess of what is nutritionally adequate but only about three-quarters the amount of protein that most Americans actually consume each day—will lead to a negative calcium balance even if the intake of dietary calcium is very high.[61] In short, it is not that we are getting too little calcium, it is that we are getting too much protein.

Myth Number Five: Small children require more protein than adults and must eat meat to ensure adequacy of protein intake.

First, it is simply not true that small children need more protein than adults. They do require more protein per body weight, but they require less protein overall. Moreover, for similar reasons as those discussed above, the protein children consume need not come from animal meat. Children in other cultures and in our own have been raised from birth as vegetarians with absolutely no negative health consequences.[62]

Indeed, it has become increasingly apparent that children in our society have begun to exhibit some of the same health problems as adult meat eaters. Children today are increasingly overweight, and suffer the initial stages of many of the diseases of affluence, particularly diabetes and partial coronary occlusion (blocking of the arteries) associated with consumption of meat. It is better, both from a physical and a psychological standpoint, to start children off on a vegetarian diet, rather than expect them to make the transition in midlife.

With scientific evidence virtually conclusive on the issue of the adequacy of the vegetarian diet, how is it that the protein myth is still so pervasive? At least part of the answer to this question has to do with whose interest is most compromised by these modern findings. In the United States, the meat industry is the second largest processing and manufacturing industry—second only to the automobile industry.[63] The dairy industry is similarly large and influential. Together, the meat lobby along with the National Dairy Council have exerted consistent attempts to manipulate the flow of information to the consumer. As merely one example of the high level of influence wielded by these groups, the meat lobby forced the Senate to debate a provision in the 1976 McGovern report on nutrition. The result of the debate: a provision encouraging consumers to "decrease consumption of meat" was altogether scrapped and replaced with the following: "Choose meat, poultry and fish which will reduce saturated fat intake." [64] Similar efforts on the part of both the meat lobby and the dairy council are well documented elsewhere.[65] There is profit, it seems, in propping up the protein myth.

Athletes and Vegetarianism

Perhaps the biggest myth of all concerning protein has yet to be considered; it is the still popular view that meat eating is necessary for optimal athletic performance. To put it another way, it is thought that vegetarianism somehow detracts from one's athletic ability by preventing the development of strength, endurance, and a variety of other qualities necessary to athletic achievement. Again, however, modern evidence and life experience prove this to be woefully inaccurate and downright false.

Perhaps, at some subliminal level, the connection between meat and sports can be traced to some primordial notion that, by eating animals, we somehow incorporate into ourselves their most valued attributes. In ancient cultures around the globe, before a big hunt, or pursuant to pagan religious rites, aspirants would consume the meat of the animal whose attributes he hoped to emulate. From the ancient Middle Eastern Mithraic bull cults, which worshiped the power and virility of the bull god, to the American Indian's belief that eating the flesh of the deer would render him fleet of foot and silent in his trek through the forests, the idea that we become what we eat appears to be a subtle, primitive and universal phenomenon.[66] (Nor is the phenomenon necessarily pagan. Some psychologists have explained even the Catholic doctrine of transubstantiation as the attempt to internalize the virtues of Christ through the eating of the bread and wine, symbolic for the "body of Christ, blood of heaven.")

Of course, if this is indeed the motivation, at some unconscious level, the traditional meaning behind the modern athlete's "cult of meat" loses its appeal. It is difficult to understand which attributes the athlete might be seeking to incorporate from the cow, the pig, or the chicken, the most likely objects of the sportsman's gustatory quest for excellence. Perhaps myths of a modern, physiological variety have replaced earlier metaphysical versions of the same.

The modern physiological myth again centers around protein and its function in the human diet. Athletes have come to associate protein, and thus meat, with physical strength and stamina. Athletes in the past were sometimes placed on "protein and water" diets by zealous trainers. The object of such dietary regimens, which obviously centered around meat to the near exclusion of all else, was to perfect the muscles and to dissolve the fat from the bodies of the athletes. Unfortunately for these athletes, this system displays a profound misunderstanding both of the function of protein and of the need for other dietary nutrients.

It is now beyond question that protein is *not* responsible for, or causally linked to, the ability to do hard work of any kind, athletic or otherwise. It is *carbohydrates*—the body's fuel—that are necessary in the course of physical exertion. The National Academy of Sciences has concluded succinctly: "There is little evidence that muscular activity increases the need for protein."[67] Protein is not eaten for strength, endurance, or performance. Rather, its function is to help build or rebuild bodily tissues, including muscles. While the building and reinforcement of muscle is undoubtedly an important aspect of athletic training and diet, an emphasis on meat is neither necessary nor helpful to the athlete for three reasons.

First, protein can be had from other dietary sources. Thus, to the extent protein is important, meat is not an essential component of the athlete's diet. Second, the importance of the muscle-building aspects of athletic training vary from sport to sport. There is obviously more of an emphasis on development of muscular bulk in weight lifting than, for example, in long-distance running. Third, and perhaps most importantly, an emphasis on protein may come at the expense of an even more important part of the diet—the need for carbohydrates. It is carbohydrates that are essential to optimal performance in tests requiring great physical exertion, particularly in the form of athletic endurance. As might be expected, vegetarians fare much better than non-vegetarians on tests and forms of competition requiring stamina.[68] In short, an emphasis on meat in the dietary regimen of most athletes will leave them lagging behind in any contest of endurance.

Numerous studies, dating from the turn of the century to the present time, have repeatedly demonstrated that endurance scores are much higher for vegetarians than for nonvegetarians. In one study, the scores of vegetarians were double those of meat eaters with respect to endurance. Further, the recovery time (from physical exhaustion) is much less for vegetarians; in one study, vegetarians took only one-fifth the time to recover from strenuous physical activity as compared with meat eaters. These findings were borne out in a Danish study in 1968, which found that vegetarians were able to pedal a bicycle 50 percent longer than those fed a mixed meat-and-vegetables diet and three times as long as those fed a pure meat diet.[69]

In *Diet for a New America*, John Robbins discusses not only these studies but also the personal accounts of numerous world-class athletes who happen to be vegetarian. These include Dave Scott, the greatest triathlete in the world, a man who responds to the myth that meat is necessary for strength by calling it "ridiculous." The list also includes Sixto Linares, who in 1985 broke the world record for the one-day triathlon (swimming 4.8 miles, cycling 185 miles and running 52.4 miles, a double marathon.) Other vegetarian athletes include Olympic gold medalist Edwin Moses, Murray Rose, perhaps the world's greatest swimmer (who has been vegetarian since the age of two), Bill Pickering who, at age 48, set the world record for swimming the English Channel, and Andreas Cahling, bodybuilder and 1980 Mr. International.[70]

Far from a justification for meat eating, the modern athlete appears to be obliged to give up meat, at least for any kind athletic contest requiring even a modicum of physical endurance. The modern physiological myth of meat must go the way of the earlier metaphysical myths.

Mental Health, Virtue Ethics, and the Case for Vegetarianism

Vegetarianism has long been associated with a particular disposition to life and to the world, with the quest for a peaceful, harmonious existence, a life lived not at the expense of other sentient beings. In the East, the adoption of a vegetarian diet is usually an essential prerequisite to spiritual pursuit, a commitment to a life lived in accordance with principles of nonviolence. Spiritual teachers have long pointed to the calming effects on the spirit associated with a meat-free diet, itself a necessary condition for inward meditation. In the West, various moral philosophies also point to a life of contemplative happiness as the goal of life. The West, however, has not as frequently observed the connection between a vegetarian diet and the pursuit of contemplative happiness, spiritual calm, or *eudamonia*, as Aristotle would have called it. Nevertheless, there is strong evidence to indicate that there is indeed a connection between one's moral and psychological health, on one hand, and one's diet, on the other.

To the extent that a connection exists between diet and psychology, in which direction does the causality flow? Do calmer, more peace-loving people tend to become vegetarians, or does adoption of a vegetarian diet tend to lead to a more balanced emotional disposition? And what psychological effects of the transition to vegetarianism might be expected, exactly?

While there may be some truth to the notion that those with certain psychological dispositions may have a greater probability of becoming vegetarian—there appear to be no studies that confirm this—it is more likely that it is a person's beliefs and commitments, not one's personality, that are responsible for the transition to a meatless diet. In essence, it is not whether one is somehow more peace-loving by nature, but whether one comes to believe that eating animals is harmful (either for the eater or for the eaten, if not both) which is instrumental in the decision to become a vegetarian.

The more interesting issue involves the claim, which is now supported by a recent survey, that the transition to a vegetarian diet may itself have profound effects upon human temperament and mental functioning regardless of one's previous beliefs, commitments, or dispositions. This survey of vegetarians supports the millennia-old view that the adoption of the vegetarian diet brings with it a variety of positive psychological—even spiritual—changes in the great majority of those who have made the switch. Some of these changes can be classified as changes in feeling-states, such as feeling more peaceful, less aggressive, or more happy.

In the survey, 89 percent of all vegetarians surveyed reported positive psychological benefits pursuant to their change in diet. These changes included an enhanced sense of moral responsibility (21 percent), feeling more peaceful and less aggressive (19 percent), a decreased sense of guilt (17 percent), an expanded sense of nature and one's place in it (16 percent), an increase in feelings of compassion for others (12 percent), an increase in feelings of happiness and well-being (12 percent), a sense of mental stability (7 percent), and a variety of cognitive changes including greater mental clarity and the ability to concentrate (6 percent).[71] The same survey recounts a variety of personal anecdotes concerning personal growth related to the transition to vegetarianism. While the subtle line between the psychological and the spiritual may be hazy, more than one-quarter of those surveyed noticed changes in what they classified as spiritual feelings upon becoming a vegetarian.

What, then, is responsible for bringing about these changes? How can diet so dramatically affect human psychology? More why should abstinence from meat have any positive affects, cognitively, emotionally, or psychologically?

First, psychologically, it is possible that giving up meat may have potent effects on one's self-image. One may feel as if one is born again, starting life anew, taking an important step toward self-purification and living a life in accordance with one's principles, rather than merely paying lip service to these same principles. A new sense of resolve and a confidence in one's own ability to make a decision and then live by it, both necessary to becoming a vegetarian in a nonvegetarian society, can have a profoundly rejuvenating effect, psychologically. Similarly, there is a kind of psychological empowerment that comes with doing what one believes to be right in the face of sometimes difficult social odds. It is not surprising that many vegetarians trace their expanded feelings of autonomy, compassion and moral awareness to their own decision to become vegetarian.

Some survey respondents also indicated a reduction in a number of negative feelings, particularly guilt. A more healthy self-image and sense of self-directedness characteristic of the transition to vegetarianism may be the surest palliative to other, negative feelings, whatever the source of these feelings. In fact, the anecdotal experiences of those who have become vegetarians bear out the fact that the transition to a meatless diet often marks a larger transition in one's lifestyle and orientation to the world and is sometimes accompanied by positive changes in other lifestyle habits and behaviors.

In addition to the psychological affects of the move to a vegetarian diet, there are undoubtedly a host of physiological reasons for some of the psychological benefits reported by many vegetarians. First, as we have seen previously in this chapter, by eliminating meat from one's diet, one also greatly reduces one's intake of a plethora of dangerous chemicals including pesticides, vermicides, growth hormones, antibiotics, and other such substances currently used in the meat industry. Though there appear to be no studies concerning the psychological affects of these chemicals on human consumers, no leap of faith is required in hypothesizing that these toxins may profoundly, if subtly, affect the state of one's mental, as well as physical, functioning. A regular diet of large amounts of pesticides, antibiotics, and growth hormones may have significant affects upon a variety of cognitive and emotional functions.

Similarly, the existence in meat of the remnants of high levels of adrenalin and other naturally occurring substances, which are released by the animal just prior to death as it witnesses the carnage before it and reacts to the threat to its own life, should not be underestimated. These chemicals, the physiological residue of what is experienced as the "fight or flight" response, are then consumed by humans when they eat the flesh of these animals. Reports of increased mental clarity, stability, alertness, and well-being reported anecdotally and in the above survey by vegetarians may be the natural result of the reduction in the diet of these various poisons.

Finally, there may well be a variety of other physiological affects of meat-eating responsible for the feeling of "heaviness" or lethargy reported by those who eat meat for the first time after a period without it. As all things that we consume affect our state of consciousness in subtle and myriad ways, meat may pose a particularly potent, if not readily appreciated, mind-altering drug for discernible physiological reasons.

In chapter 1, we discussed Aristotle's virtue ethics, the oldest of the three moral traditions in the West. Central to his theory was the idea that our *telos*—the purpose or greatest goal toward which human beings may advance—is *eudamonia*. As we have just seen, the transition to a vegetarian diet may be conducive to achieving our innate potential, or *telos*, in three different ways. First, the vegetarian diet affects us in a direct way, physiologically. Moreover, the transition to vegetarianism is often accompanied by the psychological changes described by respondents, from feelings of increased moral responsibility to enhanced feelings of compassion. This may be due both to physiological changes in the brain and nervous system and to the beneficial psychological effects of having positively changed one's life in the face of contrary social convention. Finally, both the physical and the psychological changes appear to have what might be described as moral changes upon the personality. As we gain more control over ourselves and expand our purview of moral concern, our ability to act autonomously and purposively is naturally increased.

What is most interesting is that the attainment of virtue, happiness, and optimum mental health appear to go hand in hand. Aristotle would have agreed.

"Prudence, My Dear . . ." Or, Even
an Ethical Egoist Can Be a Vegetarian

Traditional moral philosophy distinguishes between two general
motivations or reasons for performing (or refraining from) any
action: prudence and altruistic morality. While the "moral" basis
for action includes all those reasons that require taking the interest of others into account, the domain of "prudence" is the
realm of rational self-interest. The exercise of prudence requires
looking out for oneself and one's own best interests. Most moral
philosophers argue that altruism and prudence are not mutually
exclusive, but rather, that they are complementary to one another. The morally healthy individual weighs concerns for self and
others in determining which action to take.

For the ethical egoist, however, only prudence—only an interest in oneself—is relevant to any evaluation of action. (As
such, it is only for purposes of classification that egoism is considered a "moral" theory at all.) The egoist holds that what makes
an act good or bad is solely determined by whether the outcome
of the act is beneficial to the actor—to the egoist—himself; the
interests of others have no moral significance unto themselves.

Perhaps the greatest irony of our moral lives lies in the fact
that seldom do the interests of self and other coincide; very in-
frequently do altruism and egoism point in the same direction
regarding a particular action. Happily, however, one of the few
exceptions to this general rule is with respect to the issue of
health. Good health is good for the individual and for society in
general. Any practice that fosters health promotes this happy
confluence. Of course, vegetarianism does this and more.

In this chapter, we have briefly investigated some of the salutary effects of the vegetarian diet on the physical and even
mental health of the individual. We have seen that the best of
health, physical and mental, is the rightful and characteristic reward of the vegetarian diet. That which is good for the animal
is good for the individual, and that which is good for the individual is also good for society as a whole. Few decisions in our
moral life point so univocally to the same solution as the decision to become a vegetarian.

Nor do the benefits of the vegetarian diet end with the lives and well-being of the present generation, human and animal alike. The environment and, through it, the lives of future generations also will be intimately affected by our present decisions concerning our diet.

Chapter Four

The Argument from
Global Ecology

Modern meat production, both in America and around the world, is a sprawling and seemingly all-consuming enterprise. The demands of meat production upon our natural resources, and upon the environment generally, are immense. Yet the costs to the environment of our taste for meat are seldom considered by the consumer. While most Americans today are at least vaguely aware of the affects of meat eating on health, we remain profoundly unaware of the consequences of our diet upon the environment. Indeed, it is difficult to imagine us being less aware of these facts collectively than we are.

The New Ecology and the Old World Order:
A Word about the Meat Industry

For our purposes here, the most fundamental aspect of meat production is the need for the land on which to do it. Vast amounts of land are necessary not only for the grazing of animals, but for production of the huge amounts of corn, grain, soybean, and other vegetable products with which livestock are fed. Presently, as much as 90 percent of all land put to agricultural use in the United States today is utilized either for the production of live-stock—the growing, grazing, and housing of the hundreds of millions of cattle, sheep, pigs, and other common fare for the American diet—or for land used to grow the crops that will feed these animals. *Over half of the total land area of the lower forty-eight states* is used for the production of meat and diary products, again either directly, in the case of feeding and housing these animals, or indirectly, through the cultivation of feed crops.[1]

As one historian of the beef industry has put it, profitable production of beef in the New World has always depended upon cheap forage, either in the form of free grass on the open plains or inexpensive grain.[2] Furthermore, corruption, bribery, gang warfare, and outright government handouts have been an ever-present concomitant of the beef trade in the United States and elsewhere. Few consumers realize it, but producers of beef are the beneficiaries of one of the greatest government giveaways in political history. Through various ranchers' associations and through the formation in 1920 of the American Meat Institute, cattlemen and commercial meat packers have had a continuously powerful lobbying influence in Washington, D.C., and in the state capitals.

As the result of a series of federal enactments, including the Grazing Homestead Act of 1916 and the Taylor Grazing Act of 1934, vast amounts of territory in the Western states were either granted to cattlemen or leased to them for a token permit fee. As the result of the Taylor Act alone, thirty thousand ranchers today graze their cattle on three hundred million acres of public land, an area equivalent to 16 percent of the total land area of the lower forty-eight states, *or roughly the same area as the eastern seaboard states stretching from Maine to Florida.* The permit fee paid by ranchers for the use of this land is roughly 20 to 30 percent of its market value as pastureland, according to a recent government analysis. Moreover, since these grazing permits generally run with the land, they greatly increase the value of the ranchers' private property located near the public grazing land.[3]

The modern structure of the meat industry has been described as a giant "hourglass" whereby hundreds of thousands of livestock producers reach hundreds of millions of American consumers through a small handful of meat packagers.[4] The meat-packing trade has become increasingly monopolistic during the past fifty years. Between 1945 and the mid-1980s, while the demand for meat more than doubled in the United States, the number of meat producers declined by one-half.[5] Today the "big three" meat producers—IBP (Iowa Beef Packers, owned by Occidental Petroleum), Cargill-Excel, and Con-Agra—control much of the seed grain, chemical fertilizer, and slaughterhouses in the United States, a triumph of the corporate conglomerate and vertical supply structure.[6]

As the "beef trust" continues to tighten its monopolistic stranglehold on the meat industry, the demand for more land on which to raise livestock and other farm animals for slaughter proceeds unchecked. The move to greener pastures, however, is not without its consequences.

The effects of meat production on the environment are varied, but perhaps univocally disastrous. As more land is needed for grazing livestock or growing feed crops, large areas of forest are cleared away, and in most cases lost forever, all over the United States and elsewhere around the world. Deforestation leads to the erosion of topsoil, which, along with current methods of overgrazing, results in the slow and steady conversion of areas once covered with lush forests into deserts. The conversion of the Western plains in the United States into large desert areas stands as only one example of this global process. Nor are deforestation and desertification the only resulting environmental consequences. Water pollution, global warming, the destruction of the natural habitat of other species and even the displacement of large numbers of indigenous peoples around the world are all the direct result of modern meat production. We will discuss all of these issues in the following pages.

Deforestation and Desertification

The amount of land necessary to support large-scale meat production is enormous. As land is used up, a result of overgrazing and the exploitation and agricultural exhaustion of cropland used to grow feed crops, new areas of land must be put to the same purpose. This requires that forests be cleared away to make room for grazing and feed crop production. Despite conventional wisdom concerning the incursion of urban life into the natural domain—the spread of parking lots and shopping malls at the expense of wooded areas—in fact, the great majority of deforestation takes place at the behest of livestock and feed-crop producers. In the United States today, for every one acre of forest lost to roads, houses, parking lots, and shopping centers, seven

acres are lost in the process of converting forest into feedlot and
feed cropland.[7] In the United States alone, roughly 260 million
acres of forest have been lost to the cause of meat eating, a rate
of one acre every five seconds since 1967.[8] Nor has the United
States been the hardest hit in this respect. As Third World countries "beef up" their production of meat for import to the First
World, huge areas of whole countries and subcontinents have been
cut up—and cut down—in the process of deforestation. Since
1960, nearly 25 percent of the forests of Central America have
been cleared to create pastureland for cattle. In Costa Rica alone,
the process of deforestation has reached startling proportions: 80
percent of its tropical rain forest was cleared in twenty years for
cattle production. In Mexico, 37 million acres have similarly been
lost to cattle production alone. As one researcher notes, for *each
hamburger* imported from Central America, *six square yards* of
jungle must be cleared away.[9] Less than a third of the 160,000
square miles of forest that once covered Mexico and Central
America remain as the process of deforestation proceeds at a rate
that has only escalated during the past quarter century.

The process of deforestation is even more striking and tragic
in areas of the world where soil is thin and poorly suited to livestock grazing. In such cases, cattle ranchers typically resort to
slash-and-burn techniques, overgrazing patches of land for short
periods of time before exhausting the vegetation. Once this occurs, a process that is repeated every four to eight years, ranchers simply move on to new land, burning and clearing still more
forest area as they go. This process is characteristic of livestock
production in the Amazon rain forest and in various parts of
Africa.

Of course, the harm to the environment does not end with
the process of deforestation; it only begins there. As trees are
lost, they are shortly followed by the topsoil, which was once
held in place by trees and vegetation. Topsoil erosion and its
ultimate long-term consequence, desertification, are a result of a
combination of deforestation, overgrazing of land, improper irrigation techniques, and the overuse of chemical fertilizers. All of
these are characteristic concomitants of modern meat production.
An inch of topsoil requires anywhere from two hundred to one
thousand years to form under normal conditions. In the United
States, we are now losing an inch of topsoil nationwide every

sixteen years.[10] Most areas of the United States were once covered by twenty inches of topsoil. We have now destroyed, however, between a third to a half of the total amount of topsoil nationwide. In various portions of the country, we are down to as little as six inches of soil remaining in certain areas, including vast portions of the plains states.[11] For every inch of topsoil lost, grain production is reduced by 6 percent.[12] More importantly, once a certain amount of topsoil is lost, it may be lost forever as the process of desertification takes place.

Seven billion tons of topsoil are lost to erosion *each year in the United States alone*, an amount equivalent to sixty thousand pounds annually per person. This annual amount of topsoil erosion would cover an area roughly equivalent in size to the state of Connecticut.[13] Eighty-five percent of this land erosion is the result of livestock production, a consequence of both deforestation and harsh methods of overgrazing whereby ranchers graze an overabundance of livestock on an area of land too small to support the animal population.[14]

Besides deforestation and overgrazing, topsoil erosion is furthered by the overuse of chemical fertilizers utilized in feed-crop production. Each year in the United States alone, twenty million tons of chemical fertilizers are used to force the land to grow enough crops to support the large number of animals demanded by American consumers.[15] Unfortunately, not only do these toxic chemicals pose a problem to the environment generally, they also contribute to topsoil erosion.

As topsoil erosion continues, the ultimate result is the creation of vast deserts where once the land was arable. This process is most visible not only in the African Sahel, where overgrazing and inappropriate agricultural techniques have been utilized over the past half century, and where the frontline of the Sahara desert now advances three to four miles a year,[16] but in the western United States, where large areas of plains have been systematically overgrazed for over a century. Once land is rendered unto the desert, we have lost valuable cropland, we have driven other species from their natural habitat, and, as we shall see later, we have forced millions of people from rural areas of the Third World into cities, into poverty, and often into starvation. (See chapter 5.)

In sum, in order to meet the modern consumer's demands for

meat, meat producers require vast amounts of land for feed-crop production and cattle grazing. Modern meat producers both here and abroad often find it cheaper to overgraze land and move on to newer areas, rather than to take the measures necessary to preserve the land. Sixty percent of the world's grazing land has been damaged by overgrazing in the past half-century.[17]

Moreover, as trees are cut down to provide more land for feed-crop production and livestock grazing, one of the important natural elements in anchoring topsoil is lost. When this same land is overgrazed, the remaining vegetation is similarly lost. Strong winds, rain, and even the movement of cattle tear away at the surface of the earth, eroding the once-twenty-inch thin crust of soil that supports all of our agricultural needs. Overuse of the land in production of feed, improper irrigation, and increased use of chemical fertilizers also contributes to the process of topsoil erosion. As a result, in the less-affected areas, we have reduced our agricultural productivity markedly. A recent Department of Agriculture report states that the agricultural productivity of the nation's land has been reduced by 70 percent over the last two hundred years.[18] In more dramatically affected areas, as the topsoil layer dwindles into dust, once arable cropland is perhaps permanently converted to desert.

Deforestation and desertification affect us not only aesthetically, as once majestic forests are leveled and as once pristine pastureland is left for desert, and not only by strangling our agricultural capacity, but in other ways as well. A number of other environmental problems are linked to the loss of forested areas nationwide and worldwide. We shall turn to these problems shortly. Before we do, there are still other ways in which meat production dramatically and deleteriously affects the environment. Perhaps the most significant of these is the effect of livestock production on our water supply.

Meat Production and Our Water Supply

The raising and slaughter of cattle and other forms of livestock also pose a variety of unprecedented harms to our water supply. First, as we shall see, meat production represents the single most significant use of water nationwide. At a time when many areas of the nation face severe water shortages, it is truly amazing that such a great proportion of the nation's water supply is put to use in growing animals for slaughter. Second, and perhaps of greater concern, meat production is by far the largest cause of water pollution in the United States and the world. This is not to say that meat production is more significant in causing water pollution than any other particular industrial cause; rather, meat production by far outstrips *all other causes of water pollution nationwide and worldwide, combined.*

Huge amounts of water are essential both in growing the necessary feed crops to support the hundreds of millions of farm animals nationwide and the billions of animals worldwide, and for direct consumption by these same animals. As we shall see in chapter 5, meat production is tremendously wasteful in terms of our food supply: it takes a much greater amount of plantfood to feed animals that will then feed us, than it would to feed this plantfood to us directly. The same principle applies in the case of the use of water. Obviously, more water is required to raise plants with which animals are fed, and to water the animals themselves, than would be necessary to meet human needs alone on a vegetarian diet. What is not so obvious is how wasteful this process is.

When all of the uses of water necessary to meat production are summed up, 2,500 gallons of water are required to produce one pound of beef.[19] *Thus, more water goes into the production of a quarter pound hamburger than the average human drinks directly in four years.* How does this compare with the amount of water necessary to produce vegetable matter? One estimate provides that it requires anywhere from ten to one thousand times as much water to produce a pound of beef vis à vis a pound of plantfood.[20] Of course, the amount of water necessary will vary from one type of plant to the next. Overall, however, an accurate portrayal probably lies toward the low end of this estimated range. For example, roughly fifteen times as much water is necessary to produce a pound of beef as compared with a pound of soybeans.[21] Other important grains, including wheat, rice, and barley, require a similar amount of water.

In many areas of the country, battles fought between cattle ranchers and farmers have been historically significant in the shaping of the great Western realpolitik. Today these battles are viewed to have taken place over land—the ranchers' claimed right to graze their animals vis à vis the farmers' right to plant and raise crops unmolested by wandering livestock. While these land battles certainly did take place, land was not the only commodity at stake. The historical significance of water, which is sometimes overlooked today, was played out both in terms of competing claims for riparian rights and in larger, more regional battles where the politically stronger ranchers often exercised considerable control in diverting water resources from regions with more plentiful supplies. Today, some of these traditional supplies of water have run dry, either temporarily in times of drought, or permanently due to overuse of the existing reserves. Moreover, there is strong evidence that underground water reserves are running dry.[22] This poses serious long-term consequences for our water supply.

Eighty percent of our nation's total consumptive use of water goes to livestock production, either in the form of raising feed crops or for direct consumption by livestock.[23] Meanwhile, many communities now face the prospect of water rationing or, minimally, community efforts similar to those used in cities and towns across California aimed at limiting the amount of water used for everyday human consumption in homes. It is striking that 80 percent of all water used nationwide should be squandered on meat production while we ration and fight over the remaining 20 percent. It is similarly remarkable that, at a time when many areas of the nation confront the real possibility of an insufficient water supply on a permanent basis, enormous amounts of water are used in raising beef.

It is difficult to say which is worse: wasting our limited supply of water or polluting it. But water pollution is the second way meat production has affected the water supply—and it has affected it in a significant way.

The culprit, in this case, is animal waste. The average 1,100 pound steer produces forty-seven pounds of manure every twenty-four hours.[24] One source estimates that cattle alone produce nearly one billion tons of organic waste (that's 2,000,000,000,000 pounds) each year worldwide while another states that all farm animals together produce about twice this amount.[25] Each year, the total amount of this waste produced weighs over four times as much as the combined weight of the human population of the entire planet. That's each year. Where does all this waste go?

That's the problem.

Most of this nitrogenous waste turns into soluble compounds of ammonia and nitrates that leach through the ground and contaminate the groundwater. Or it runs off into the surface water, polluting lakes, rivers, and streams. As these compounds seep into the water supply, they promote algae growth that in turn depletes the water of oxygen. As the water is deoxygenated, aquatic life dies. Of course, the water itself is rendered unusable once it has been contaminated in this fashion.

Livestock production also contributes to water pollution in another way. After animals are slaughtered, unusable portions of the animals' bodies, along with grease and other by-products of the modern, streamlined killing process, are dumped into rivers, lakes, or dry-waste areas where they decompose and, again, contaminate the groundwater and surface water through runoff of the material.

Altogether, the toll on our nation's water supply is staggering. Animal dung alone causes *twice* the water pollution *of all other industrial causes of water pollution combined.*[26] Add to this the other effects of meat production, including the dumping of body parts, animal viscera, and grease, and it is clear that meat eating may be responsible for as much as 80 percent of all water pollution.

We have stated here that 80 percent of all consumptive use of water in our nation goes to raising animals. Further, as much as 80 percent of all water pollution is also tied to meat production. If we, as a nation, were to give up eating meat tomorrow, this could have absolutely rejuvenating effects upon the nation's (and the world's) water supply.

If everyone in America were to become a vegetarian tomorrow and if all meat production stopped, 80 percent of the water we now put to livestock production would be freed for other uses. The remaining 20 percent is currently put to use in growing fruits and vegetables for direct human consumption and for other consumptive uses including providing water for drinking and cooking. Even if the move to a vegetarian diet required us to increase by 50 percent the amount of water now used for nonmeat related purposes (from 20 to 30 percent)—this extra water would presumably be used to grow additional vegetable matter to replace the meat in our diets—we still would require only 30 percent of the consumptive use of water now necessary to feed a nation of meat eaters. In short, a nationwide move to vegetarianism would cut by more than two-thirds the amount of water now used for all consumptive purposes.

In addition, water pollution would be greatly reduced. Not only would we eliminate the cause of as much as four-fifths of all water pollution, but the significantly reduced burden on agricultural land would permit farmers to abjure the use of fertilizers, another cause of groundwater contamination. In short, if we were to stop all meat production tomorrow, both the quantity and the quality of our nation's—and our world's—water supply would be tremendously enhanced.

Meat Production and the Destruction of Other Species

The modern taste for meat contributes to the displacement or outright destruction of other animal species in six distinct ways. Most directly, of course, we must kill the animals we eat. As we have noted previously, this results in the premeditated extermination of literally billions of animals a year—from fish to poultry to higher mammals including sheep, pigs, and, in some cultures, whales, dolphins, and monkeys. As humans can live even healthier lives with a vegetarian diet than by eating meat, all this carnage is simply unnecessary, both morally and from the standpoint of health. In five other indirect ways, we also contribute to the displacement, even the extinction, of other animal species.[27]

First, in hunting certain species, other species may be inadvertently harmed in the process. The most obvious example of this is the destruction of dolphins and whales who migrate with tuna and are often caught in the nets of tuna fishermen. Thousands of whales and dolphins die each year as the result of tuna fishing, a fact made all the more deplorable by the fact that dolphins and whales are probably the most intelligent animals on earth after humans.

Second, as more land is converted to use for cattle grazing and feedcrop production, other animals are displaced, fenced out of their natural habitat, driven to compete with other animals for increasingly less space. In the western United States, species of elk, deer, and bighorn sheep have been systematically fenced out of wide pasture areas they once roamed freely. Many such animals have simply starved to death. Others are driven into intense competition with members of their own species and those of other species for correspondingly smaller areas. Moreover, the use of pesticides and chemical defoliants used to clear previously uncultivated areas further endanger these animals. Many of these species face extinction as nature is pushed to the breaking point, with too little food and too little space to permit the continued existence of many individuals and increasingly more species.

A third way in which meat production indirectly but palpably affects other animals takes place via the destruction of riparian habitat as the result of cattle grazing. As cattle graze near the banks of streams and rivers, they inadvertently kick large chunks of land into these waterways. When this happens, rivers tend to become wider and shallower. As a result, the temperature of the water heats up, in some cases dramatically. In many instances, the waterways simply dry up altogether. Whether as the result of the raised temperature, the shallower water depths, or the outright evaporation of these bodies of water, a variety of forms of aquatic life are endangered or have been destroyed. Nor is the gravity of this problem marginal. With 29 percent of the total land area of the United States put to use for cattle grazing, the problem is an immense one, all the more troubling when we consider that much of this land is overgrazed and cannot, without severe consequences, support the cattle population on the land. One commentator on the subject cites a 1988 General Accounting Office report that states that "poorly managed livestock grazing is the major cause of degraded riparian habitat on federal rangelands."[28]

Deforestation to clear land for livestock production accounts for the fourth way in which the modern taste for meat leads to the destruction of other species. As trees are cleared away, not only is the habitat of tree-dwelling animals destroyed, but the ecological foundation for a complex chain of life is irretrievably swept away. Other species of plants and animals are affected by the loss of tree cover and the land-anchoring effect of tree roots. As we have seen, as trees are destroyed, topsoil erosion follows. As each link in the chain of life is affected by these changes, so too are other links that depend upon them. This is particularly true in densely forested areas and in jungles. For example, in the Amazon rain forest, a region that has recently witnessed deforestation at an unprecedented rate, it is estimated that over 15 percent of all plant species on earth could be lost forever.[29] The significance of this becomes apparent when we consider that many of these species of plants are necessary for the production of various forms of medicine and other products beneficial to humans, and that many of these species are exclusively indigenous to the Amazon region. Further, since we are only beginning to understand and recognize all of the various forms of plant life found in the Amazon, along with the benefits they may hold for humans, we may never fully appreciate the extent of our loss due to the destruction of the Amazon rain forest.

The fifth way in which the meat culture affects the lives of other species of animals is perhaps the most pernicious of all; it is simultaneously a cause and an effect of our behavior toward other species generally. The meat culture engenders an *attitude* toward other animals—an attitude that says we can do as we wish with other animals, whether that means killing them or making them our pets. It is this attitude that, subtly and, at times, overtly, poses the gravest consequences for the environment. We will return to this issue in the last section of this chapter.

It has been argued by some writers that calls for the abolition of hunting, as well as for the moral obligatoriness of vegetarianism, ignore our status as participants and competitors in the ecological system. Not only do we have a right to hunt, kill, displace various species or otherwise have an effect on the natural world as we so choose, this view maintains, but we possess a kind of "natural duty" to do so. Thus, a concern with other species, some writers argue, is misplaced, even unnatural. One naturalist writer contends: "A condemnation of hunting, while advocating vegetarianism, has been made . . . [But this fails] to understand the human role as a participant in the system. Participating in the ecological scheme implies surviving within it, and to survive humans must successfully compete for its resources. . . . Thus, to participate in the global ecology, humans must eat. If we kill other animals, that is one form of participation."

The argument concludes by claiming that "the position of universal vegetarianism can only be argued from positions of ignorance regarding global ecology or of naive interpretations of ecological realities."[30] It is this argument, however, which is argued from the position of ignorance—in this case, an ignorance of logic.

The argument is a familiar one. It assumes that "competing with" other animals—in other words, killing them, directly or indirectly—is "natural," an essential aspect of the natural order. In chapter 6, we will examine the argument that meat eating is natural because killing and death are a part of the natural scheme of things. For now, however, we will limit ourselves to examining the claim that vegetarianism, with its emphasis on the interests of other animals, fails to understand our role in the global ecology.

Humans have been very effective competitors—too effective, it seems, for our own good. Indeed, we may ultimately compete ourselves right out of the ecological order. But the "argument from natural competition," as we might call it, is logically unsound. It might be represented as follows:

1. To participate in the ecosystem, humans must compete.

2. To compete successfully, humans must eat.

3. Meat eating is one form of participation in the ecological system.

Therefore, either advocating vegetarianism or condemning hunting on grounds that it is wrong to kill animals fails to understand global ecology or is a "naive interpretation" of "ecological realities."

This argument is logically invalid. Even if it is true that eating meat is one form of participating in the ecological system, it is not the *only* way to do so nor, as we have seen, is it the best way to do so from an ecological perspective. Thus, it is simply not true that advocating vegetarianism is naive or unrealistic. Indeed, as we have seen, an end to modern meat production may become ecologically unavoidable at some point in the not-so-distant future.

The proponent continues with the second oft-proposed aspect of the "argument from natural competition." It holds, most basically, that vegetarianism poses a greater threat to the environment and to other species than do meat eating and meat production:

> Moreover, the level of crop production necessary to support humans as vegetarians necessarily involves competition with animals of other species. Usually, the competition is well defined in terms of competition with individual members of species; rather, whole species tend to be adversely influenced, usually being completely displaced by the crop production necessary to achieve the aims of vegetarianism.[31]

The argument here is simply predicated on a false premise—an assumption that, as we have already seen, turns out to turn reality on its head. The writer assumes that crop production would be *higher* for a vegetarian culture than for a nation of meat eaters. This ignores, however, the fact that, in this nation alone, we currently have to feed hundreds of millions of head of livestock many of which weigh more than five times as much as the average human being. Needless to say, we would require substantially less crop production to feed 240 million vegetarians weighing, on average, between 150 and 200 pounds, than would be necessary to feed the 112 million beef cattle (weighing 1,100 pounds each), the 85 million hogs (weighing 200 to 300 pounds each), the 9 million sheep (weighing 100 to 150 pounds each) and the 3.3 billion chickens, which are consumed in the United States alone each year, *plus* the required supplemental plant food of the same 240 million human omnivores.[32]

The unmistakable truth is that the level of crop production would be dramatically reduced—by at least a factor of four, assuming a direct correlation between the amount of plantfood needed and the combined weight of the humans and animals in the figures above—if we were, as a nation, to embrace a vegetarian diet. Today, 90 percent of all land put to agricultural use is used for meat production.[33] Returning even half of this land to natural use would mean a significantly lowered rate of displacement of other species. Thus, both aspects of the "argument from natural competition" fail, the first as a matter of pure logic, and the second by virtue of a false premise.

Meat production and meat eating require not only the killing of hundreds of millions of animals a year nationwide and billions of animals each year globally, they result in the displacement and destruction of still other animal species. This occurs when other species are killed as an incident to fishing or hunting. The level of crop production necessary to feed the hundreds of millions of head of livestock in this nation alone, along with the pastureland needed for grazing, entail that increasingly large tracts of land need to be fenced off, thereby displacing other species from large areas of their former habitat. The result has been intensely increased competition for ever-dwindling natural resources and, in many cases, the death of large numbers of animals and the endangerment of entire species.

Moreover, as more forests are cleared away for these purposes, still other plant and animal life is endangered, top-soil erosion takes place, and the intricate balance of life dependent upon the harmonious, if barbarous, interaction of these various species is similarly affected. Thus, each ecological consequence moves out like a ripple in a pond, affecting widely varying species as they interact in the Great Chain of Being, each influence reinforcing the others, and itself being influenced by the others. As certain species dwindle, become extinct, or are driven further from their previous habitat, the effects on still other species become apparent. Many of these events portend widespread, frightening, if not entirely predictable, results for the plant and animal world, for the global environment—and for humankind itself.

Other Environmental Problems
Related to Mass Meat Production

There exist two other long-term environmental problems related to mass meat production. First, raising livestock contributes to the process of global warming. Global warming, sometimes called the "greenhouse effect," takes place when the ozone layer traps greater amounts of terrestrial heat than normal, radiating it back to the earth. Life on earth is possible because a certain amount of heat is trapped by gases in the ozone layer, which permits the earth to retain some of the heat necessary for the development of life as we know it on our planet. When additional gases are added to this layer, however, greater amounts of heat (which is basically long wavelength infrared radiation) are reflected back to earth, further heating up the surface temperature of the planet. The offending gases, those most responsible for global warming, are carbon dioxide, nitrous oxide, methane, and chlorofluorocarbons, along with a number of less-significant trace gases.[34]

Global warming has already affected the planet by increasing the average temperature worldwide by 0.7 degrees Celsius (over 1 degree Fahrenheit). Unless abated, the greenhouse effect will continue to raise the temperature of the planet at an average of 0.3 degrees Celsius every decade.[35] This is the *average* worldwide affect; in fact, temperatures will rise more significantly the further one moves from the equator, with correspondingly less variation at the equator. Thus, while the entire planet could warm anywhere between 1.5 to 4.5 degrees Celsius (roughly 3 to 8 degrees Fahrenheit) globally by the middle of the next century, the warming could be two to three times this amount at higher latitudes.[36] Thus, in the extreme northern and southern zones of the planet, temperatures may rise twenty degrees or more.

The worldwide results of global warming, if left unchecked, will be profound and devastating. First, the variation in temperature will force many species of trees and other forms of vegetation to migrate northward in the Northern Hemisphere. Even a one-degree Celsius variation in temperature shifts temperature zones one hundred miles to the north. At the present rate, we can expected a 2 degree Celsius increase by the year 2030. But because the warming affect will take place at a rate five to ten times faster than the thaw after the last ice age, many forms of vegetation will not be able to migrate quickly enough and will die in the more extreme heat of their earlier habitat.[37] Of course, even as vegetation does migrate, so too will the animal life that depends upon it. Between the extinction of certain forms of plants and animals and the migration of others, the overall affect on global ecology, and the speed with which it will take place, will be unprecedented in biological history.

Global warming will also have a profound affect upon weather patterns and will raise sea level worldwide. The jet stream and other macroweather forces may be altered dramatically. Further, as the worldwide temperature rises, the Arctic and Antarctic ice caps will begin to thaw. A rise of four degrees Celsius will result in an ice-free Arctic ocean and the melting of the great Antarctic ice sheets with an overall rise in sea level of six meters.[38] This, of course, would have incalculably devastating affects upon many islands and such low-lying areas as the Netherlands.

Global warming would also affect weather patterns in varying ways in different areas. A rise of just 2 or 3 degrees Celsius worldwide would bring about extremely hot weather in certain areas of the nation and the world. For example, the number of days on which the temperature rises to over 100 degrees Fahrenheit would increase from one to twelve in Washington D.C., from three to twenty-one in Omaha, Nebraska, and from nineteen to seventy-eight in Dallas, Texas.[39]

Given even this cursory scenario of the effects of global warming, it is clear that the greenhouse effect poses a threat to the ecosystem and global economy second only to nuclear war. But how does meat eating contribute to global warming?

In two ways, our taste for meat contributes to the greenhouse effect. First, global warming is the result of deforestation. We have already seen that the need for land to raise livestock and grow feed crops is a major cause of deforestation. The release of carbon dioxide into the atmosphere is the major cause of the greenhouse effect, accounting for one-half of the problem of global warming. As trees are burned, they release their store of carbon into the atmosphere. Deforestation leads to the release of one to three billion metric tons of carbon into the atmosphere worldwide, annually.[40] The other major cause of this release of carbon into the atmosphere, the burning of fossil fuels, is responsible for releasing approximately six billion tons of carbon into the atmosphere. Thus, from 14 to 33 percent of all excess carbon in the atmosphere is linked to deforestation.

The second way in which global warming indirectly results

from our demand for meat is a by-product of the digestive process of livestock. Livestock produce and emit into the atmosphere
large quantities of methane. Excess methane in the atmosphere
is caused by a variety of factors including rice paddy emissions,
decomposition of vegetable matter, emissions from swamps,
marshes, and bogs and even emissions from termites.[41] Methane
from animal sources, most of which are livestock, account for
between 9 and 35 percent of all excess methane released into
the atmosphere.[42] While this relative contribution of animal digestive gases to the accumulation of atmospheric methane may
seem somewhat insignificant, it should be noted that even a small
change in the amount of methane in the atmosphere has a large
affect upon global warming. This is because the absorption band
of methane is large; thus, a small amount of methane reflects a
large amount of infrared radiation back to earth.[43]

Finally, it should be noted that many of these factors have
reinforcing influences upon one another. For example, as more
carbon is released into the atmosphere, the amount of methane
production from decaying vegetation is also increased.[44] Similarly, reduced summer soil moisture, itself a product of the greenhouse effect, results in the loss of freshwater wetlands, streams,
and rivers and the lowering of underground aquifers.[45] Thus, the
greenhouse effect will contribute to our shortage of water. In sum,
there are no effects that do not, in turn, have other effects upon
planetary ecology. All of nature is delicately balanced and intimately intertwined.

In addition to global warming, the second general consequence
of modern meat production is "environmental" only in the most
extended and tragic sense of the term. As land is cleared of trees,
overcultivated and overgrazed, it is robbed of its agricultural
capacity. This not only affects other species, but also forces those
who once lived on the land to move on to "greener pastures."
Hundreds of millions of people in vast regions of the Third World
live on land ravaged by the process of desertification, a disaster
that has turned countless millions into refugees. As, the Independent Commission on International Human Issues found, the
effects of drought and desertification only serve to further widen
the gap, forcing millions in such areas as the African Sahel into
urban areas where they are worse off than ever before.[46]

The long-term and widespread consequences of mass meat production are enormous on our environment, and on the rural poor of many areas of the world. In the next chapter, we will consider at length the effects of worldwide meat production on the problem of world hunger.

From Christian Eschatology to the Gaia Hypothesis: Extroverting Our Ethics

In the West, we are unaccustomed to the notion that we have ethical obligations to, or in virtue of, plants, animals, or the natural world. The influence of Christianity, in this respect as in others, has been substantial. In contrast to native American religion or to most Eastern religions, which stress the need for our harmonious coexistence with the nonhuman world, the Western worldview has led to human dominion, domination and exploitation of the nonhuman world. Where Eastern and nativist religions hold that humankind is merely part of the cosmic pattern, a single element in the web of all life, Western religion, morality and law place humans at the apex of worldly creation; moreover, the Western worldview, itself influenced by Christian eschatology, generally entails that everything else in the natural domain is not only morally subordinate to humans in the cosmic order but also has been put here for us to do with as we choose.

Christian morality has placed emphasis historically on the cultivation of the spirit to the exclusion of virtually all else. Christian dualism, as it developed under the influence of Augustine and the Neoplatonic church fathers, contrasts the immortal soul with the decaying and dying body, and the spiritual domain with the material world, including the natural world. Correspondingly, the moral domain was almost exclusively limited to the pursuit of otherworldly salvation, either through the cultivation of the virtues, through the development of faith, or by the pursuit of good works (generally, with notable exceptions such as St. Francis, directed only to other human beings).

The natural world simply did not have moral standing under the Christian worldview for two related reasons. First, in what was perhaps partially the result of the Christian reaction to the pananimism of certain pre-Christian religions, which Christianity sought to displace and vanquish, the church decided early on that animals (not to mention plants) did not possess immortal souls. (See chapter 2 for a discussion of this.) Thus, humans had no particular moral or religious obligations to either plants or animals though, again, some theologians contended that humans should be kind to animals on the view that animals were capable of feeling pain.

Second, because Christian eschatology held that the end of the world was imminent, ethical concerns were "driven inward," away from the world at large.[47] If the world was a place of irredeemable imperfection, even evil, cast off and separated from the divine by the almost insuperable gulf created by the Fall, then surely there was no point in salvaging it. Souls were saved; worlds were not. Thus, we had no obligations concerning the natural world—even to the future generations who might otherwise have been affected by this same waste and exploitation of the world's resources.

Modern Western moral philosophy has followed the lead of Christian dualism, even where it has purported to be predicated upon rational, rather than theological, foundations. Thus, the Western philosophical tradition over the course of the past three centuries has basically followed the Cartesian dichotomy between mind and body. Thus, the same basic dichotomy is played out with the same resulting implications: not only do we have no moral obligations to, or in virtue of, the natural world, but plants and animals themselves are completely excluded from the domain of moral consideration, both as moral agents and as subjects of moral rights. (Indeed, while Kant argued for an end to cruelty to animals, it was solely on the ground that human cruelty to animals makes humans more cruel *to each other*, a proposition that may be true but is only marginally relevant.)

While the modern moral philosopher converted sins to vices, and even as obligations to God were transformed into natural (human) rights, the *object* of morality remained basically the same. Lying, promise breaking, incontinence, and intemperance of various forms remained the focus of moral analysis, at least until the rise of utilitarianism changed the emphasis of morality from the personal to the social consequences of an action. Nevertheless, throughout this period, while telling a lie might leave

one's immortal soul in mortal jeopardy or, minimally, subject one
to the criticism that she was acting in violation of the most fundamental social or moral principles, one could burn down an
(unowned) forest with virtual impunity.

The recognition that the natural world matters, morally—that
"trees have standing" as one legal scholar has put it—is a recent
phenomenon. It began in earnest with increasing evidence that
animals experience thoughts and emotions in ways that are not
fundamentally different from the way humans do, and has continued, during the past twenty years, with the environmental
movement and the growing abundance of scientific evidence that
demonstrates that the way we treat the natural world *does* matter. The Gaia hypothesis, developed and articulated by James
Lovelock and Lynn Margulis, is perhaps the fullest expression
to date of the view that nature matters and that all forms of life
on earth are dependent not only upon each other, but also upon
climatic conditions generally.

The Gaia hypothesis has sometimes been misconstrued. "Gaia"
was the term used by the ancient Greeks to personify the earth.
Lovelock adopted the term when he hypothesized that the entire
earth is a giant homeostatic, self-regulating, self-contained system. The hypothesis holds that climatic conditions have had, and
continue to have, discernible and dramatic influences upon the
course of evolution. As the climate regulates life, so life exerts
a reciprocal influence upon the climatic conditions and the environment generally. The entire planet is thus viewed as a "bio-
sphere," a self-interactive "adaptive control system."[48] As the
climate goes, so goes the general course of evolution. And, reciprocally, as dominant forms of life change on the planet, this
has an affect upon the climate itself, as when a proliferation of
plant life creates more oxygen in the atmosphere. Thus, the living world and its environment continually interact and regulate
each other, not in some purposive or teleological fashion as some
have misconstrued it, but as the result of determinate, scientific
laws.

Gaia is not only a scientific hypothesis concerning the interdependence of all aspects of the biosystem, it stands as a meta-
phor for our own interdependence with the environment, and for
the intimate relationship between the way in which we live and

our effects upon the world around us. It stands for our need to
harmoniously live within the natural order, rather than attempting to subjugate that order to our own limited whims. It points
to the need for us to extrovert our ethics, to include the natural
world in the domain of ethical consideration, if not for the natural world itself, then for the consequences of a changed world
to ourselves. It attests to the fact that the results of deforestation
and desertification, the destruction of our water supply, global
warming, and the impact of all of these activities upon other
species will ultimately come back to us.

   Indeed, they already have come back to us. In discussing the
great African famine of the mid-1980s, some of the most significant causes of which include the same processes of deforestation and desertification we have discussed throughout this
chapter, the Independent Commission on International Human
Issues stated:

> It is our considered opinion that what is happening in Africa today
> can very well happen in other parts of the globe tomorrow. As
> forests retreat and deserts advance, as threats to essential life sup-
> port systems increase and ecological fragility grows, so will the
> vulnerability of the human race. If man continues in the profligate
> use of resources and to struggle against nature instead of cooperat-
> ing with it to improve the quality of life, no continent may be spared
> the kind of problem now facing Africa.[49]

Chapter Five

The Argument from World Hunger

With the growing ecological consciousness that has steadily developed over the course of the past two decades or so, we have begun to see the important connections between patterns of food production and consumption in the wealthy, developed countries and those in the developing world. In her classic work, *Diet for a Small Planet*, Frances Moore Lappé made an impressive case for the connection between meat eating in the First World and the gross waste of food resources here and abroad. More specifically, she argued that a significant percentage of the total world output of grain is being used as cattle feed. Thus, cattle are fed with the same grain that could fend off starvation for millions of people around the globe. As Jeremy Rifkin has written, "a third of the world's grain harvest is now being fed to cattle and other livestock while nearly a billion human beings go to bed malnourished."[1]

Moreover, the same land that cattle graze upon could similarly be put to better use—namely, for the development of agricultural products with which we might feed the world. Together, the argument runs, the use of grain and arable land for the production of meat constitute a grossly culpable misuse of the limited resources of our planet. This misuse takes on the proportions of a kind of mass reckless homicide on the international level when we consider the plight of hundreds of millions of others who are starving and who might be saved by proper use of these same resources.

Lappé and many others have responded by calling for a move in the developed world and elsewhere to a vegetarian diet. Some have marshaled impressive figures to make the point. One writer on agricultural economics states, "Although the unfair distribution which characterizes international trade makes it an unlikely dream, it is also a fact that if everyone in the developed world became a vegetarian, it would be possible to give four tons of edible grain to every starving person."[2]

Here, we will consider the argument from world hunger in the context of contemporary political and economic conditions. I will argue that various writers have tended to oversimplify the connection between meat eating and world hunger. While adoption of the vegetarian diet on a widescale basis will have a salutary effect on our ability and willingness to feed the malnourished around the planet, the reasons for this are rather more complex and indirect than those suggested by some writers.

Forty Thousand Children Every Day: An Overview of Worldwide Famine and Malnutrition

It is a well-known if little understood phenomenon: human comprehension of human misery varies inversely with the magnitude of the disaster. The greater the calamity, the less likely we are to feel compassion, sympathy, motivation to do anything about it. Each night on the television news, stories of small-scale tragedy touch the hearts and lives of millions of viewers. The baby in need of the liver transplant, the newlyweds killed in an automobile accident, the victims of an accidental fire—all these are personal stories that we react to on an individual basis. We react because we learn about the individuals, we empathize with them, and because the tragedy may have been prevented. Meanwhile, tragedy on the large scale takes on the air of statistical unreality. Tragedy in small numbers affects *people*, but tragedy in the thousands or even millions is merely a fact. Indeed, it does not even make for good tragedy.

So it is with worldwide famine and malnutrition. The facts are perhaps so overwhelming, the people so distant, and the numbers so large that we choose instead to concentrate, to the extent we care to look at all, on the little tragedies. The ones we can *feel* something—and perhaps *do* something—about. Still, the facts *are* tragic: Ten percent of the world's population, over one-half billion people, do not have enough to eat. UNICEF and the World Health Organization estimate that 550 million people now suffer from a chronic lack of food.[3] Another 10 percent, slightly better off, live on the edge of starvation. Living from season to season and from crop to crop, they are in constant risk of hunger.[4] Forty to sixty million people, a number equivalent to fully a fifth of the population of the United States, die each year of hunger and hunger-related diseases.[5] Hundreds of millions of others live in conditions of abject misery.

The hardest hit, of course, are the children. Around the world, forty thousand children die hunger-related deaths each day.[6] Imagine an epidemic that struck only the largest university towns, a different town every day, killing in one day all of the enrolled students before moving on to yet another town the following day. Deaths from such an epidemic would barely keep pace with those that actually occur from worldwide famine though, of course, the famine deaths are more diffuse, the numbers more scattered, and those who die in reality are much younger. More children die of starvation every two to three months than people have died to date worldwide as a result of the AIDS virus. Fourteen million children under the age of five die every year of malnutrition and related diseases.[7] Nor are the great majority of these the result of famine, as we have come to understand the term. Rather, these are the victims of chronic hunger. Even in the best of times, for example, malnutrition kills one thousand Ethiopian children every day.[8] Thousands of children die similar deaths in many parts of the world, particularly Asia, Africa, and Latin America. When it occurs, famine only aggravates an already desperate situation.

A comparison of the dietary intake in the developed and developing nations reveals that, on average, people in the First World consume six times as much milk, eggs, and other dairy products as do those in the Third World. We eat four times as much meat, fat, and oils. Our average caloric intake per day is 3,150 calories as compared with 2,200 calories in the developing nations. Each day, people in the developing nations seldom achieve the minimum amount of protein necessary to live while those in the developed nations consume more than twice the protein they will need.[9] And even these statistics are misleading because, within and between the various developing countries there is great variation in nutritional intake. These figures are merely the average for all persons in all developing countries taken together. The one billion human beings who represent the poorest of the poor fare even worse than our numbers may suggest, some consuming as little as 1,500 calories a day, a dangerously inadequate amount.[10]

Those who die each year of hunger and its attendant evils number in the millions. But the hundreds of millions who live in conditions of "absolute poverty"—poverty by any standard, poverty beyond the very comprehension of those in wealthier nations—face a plethora of diseases, social ills, and related miseries. Life under these conditions truly mirrors Thomas Hobbe's state of nature, a life "nasty, brutish and short." According to Robert McNamara, president of the World Bank, those living under such conditions have an infant mortality rate eight times higher than that of the developed nations, a life expectancy at least one-third lower, an adult literacy rate 60 percent less and, as we have seen, a nutritional level that is often simply inadequate to sustain life.[11]

Nor is it necessarily the case that people in the poorest countries are simply victims of their own economic underproduction. In some cases, this is true, of course, but only in a surprisingly small number of countries.[12] In other cases, a variety of political and economic factors, including escalating international debt and trade deficits, force countries to export food at higher prices, rather than feed their own. In crop year 1889-90, nations in Africa, Asia, and Latin America collectively produced more than one-half the grain grown worldwide. These countries were responsible for growing 95 percent of the rice, 42 percent of the wheat, and 34 percent of other grains such as millet and sorghum.[13] Nevertheless, in the wake of colonialism, Africa, Asia, and Latin America have gone from grain-exporting to grain-importing countries such that, for the first time in 1981, developing countries became net importers of agricultural products.[14]

It is sometimes argued that the developed world, and particularly the United States, is doing its share to give food aid to the developing world. In fact, the United States typically uses food aid in a—pardon the pun—carrot-and-stick approach to spread its influence economically and politically. Famine relief is frequently tied to the needy country's willingness to adhere to our economic and political agenda. For example, in 1985, more than half of American famine assistance went to just five countries in Africa: Kenya, Liberia, Somalia, Sudan, and Zaire. Twenty other nations simply went without much assistance.[15]

Nor is the amount of aid we tender to the poorer nations particularly earth shattering. The U.N. has set a goal of 0.7 percent of GNP as the amount the developed nations should seek to give in famine assistance to the Third World. Few countries have met the standard. The United States is low on the list, giving about 0.22 percent of its annual GNP in aid. Meanwhile, roughly 5 percent of our GNP goes to alcohol consumption while another 3 percent is spent on tobacco products, a combined total nearly forty times greater than the amount given in famine assistance and over ten times greater than the modest U.N. target for such assistance.[16]

But should any of this matter? If rich countries live well, what complaint do the poorer countries have? Why should we feed the starving? It is to these issues that we now turn.

Our Third World and Our First Priority: Ethical Arguments For and Against Feeding the Starving

There are plenty of psychological reasons why individuals and governments of the wealthier nations do not do more to remedy a crisis of such catastrophic proportions. The lack of geographical proximity and the sheer number of those affected often preclude the sense of individual tragedy and personal empathy that sometimes seem to be emotionally necessary in motivating a response. But is there a moral justification for our inattention?

Generally, there are two types of responses made to the claim that we ought to feed the starving or, indeed, help the needy in any country, including our own. The first is a general moral demurrer to the effect that, though malnutrition and its attendant miseries are unfortunate, the better-off have no particular obligation to set the situation right (though it might be nice of them to do so). The second is a more practical objection. It provides that helping the poor now only puts off the problem. Feeding the poor today will only lead to still more overpopulation and an even greater crisis in the future. If both of these objections can be answered satisfactorily, clearly no good reason will remain for our continued inattention to the millions starving today.

The first objection to the claim that we have an obligation to help others has been cast in a variety of different forms, philosophically. A traditional deontologist of a politically conservative orientation might argue that we possess the duty to avoid doing harm to others—a duty of nonmalificence—but *not* a duty to do affirmative good—a duty of beneficence. Thus, we have a duty not to rob a person, but we do not possess a duty to give our own money to the poor. (This philosophy, of course, tends to reinforce the status quo, economically.) It is morally commendable when someone gives charitably, but doing so is, so to speak, above and beyond the call of duty.

The criminal law, of course, generally observes this distinction between not doing wrong and doing affirmative good. Cast in the principle that one is generally only legally responsible for one's *acts* and not for one's *omissions* (except where under a specific duty to act), this doctrine is the legacy of an era of individualism and a recognition, on the part of judges and lawmakers, that the law had enough to do in preventing acts of affirmative violence. The promotion of positive good could be left for some future (presumably, utopian) time.

Thus, according to this view, as long as we, in the wealthier countries, are not responsible for the suffering of millions in the Third World—as long as we have not caused their suffering—we have no particular obligation to help. No doubt, many historians and others might claim that those living in the First World are indeed the beneficiaries of past injustice perpetrated against the ancestors of those living in the Third World, the modern legacy of imperialism, colonialism, and, in some cases, slavery. But, leaving this controversy to the side for the moment, if we are not directly responsible for their plight, neither do we have the duty to make things right.

The modern libertarian makes the same point by arguing that the poor, whether in the Third World or here at home, have no right to a redistribution of wealth of any kind as long as they have not been unjustly impoverished (e.g., cheated by fraud or victims of coercion). For the libertarian, all rights are negative, not positive—that is, there are only rights not to be interfered with, but not rights to affirmative assistance by others.[17] Thus, while developing countries have a (negative) right not to be interfered with in their internal matters, the Third World has no (positive) *right* to the money or other affirmative assistance of the First World. If the First World does lend assistance, it may do so in the amount and under any conditions it specifies. This amounts to the same thing, as a practical matter, as the deontologist's claim that the First World has no particular *duty* to the Third World, though from the "rights," rather than the "duty," side of the coin.

But is this true? Are we morally justified in pursuing a course of minimal or even nonintervention? Peter Singer has argued that our lack of support for the millions who are slowly starving to death is analogous to a person who observes a child drowning in a shallow pond.[18] The witness could easily become rescuer with no risk to himself by simply wading in and pulling the child out. Analogously, a relatively small amount of assistance could save millions, even if it might not be sufficient to save all malnourished people for all time.

Surely the failure to rescue the child would amount to an utter disregard for the life of another—a moral aloofness so crass, an omission so culpable that it is almost as condemnable as if the witness had pushed the child into the water in the first place. How is our inattention to the problem of the millions who starve each year for want of an adequate diet any different?

There are differences between the two situations, of course. But it is not clear that these differences are morally relevant— that they warrant such disparate treatment at our hands. First, of course, the drowning child is an identifiable person while those starving overseas are rather more nameless, faceless numbers to us. While this makes a *psychological* difference—it is easier to be motivated by the plight of an actual person whom we can help directly—it is not clear that this amounts to a relevant *moral* difference. Both parties are equally in danger and both could be spared by our affirmative act of kindness. There are no other relevant moral considerations. Why, then, should we assist the drowning child while ignoring the starving child (or adult)?

Second, it is always gratifying to see the good we have done in the world. In the case of the drowning child, the result and the emotional reward for having done a good thing are immediate: the rescuer has directly taken part in the act and can see the benefits. This is not the case for the person who gives money, donates time, or (as we shall discuss shortly) becomes a vegetarian for the purpose of preventing starvation in Ethiopia, for example. The effects are too attenuated; we cannot experience directly the good we have done.

Again, however, while these considerations explain why, as a psychological matter, the person of even meager moral ambitions will save the drowning child while the otherwise good-hearted may forego the opportunity to save the starving child overseas, they do not appear to make any moral difference. The only truly relevant moral considerations are that one person desperately needs help while another can easily give it.

Another difference between the two situations is that there is a sense of helplessness that comes with confronting a disaster of such catastrophic proportions. The would-be donor may despair of giving money or time to save a few persons while so many others continue to starve, or where even the present recipients may again be in trouble at a future time. Why bother? It is all like drops of water in the ocean. The sheer enormity of the tragedy tends to overwhelm the responsive sentiments, leaving a perennially unsatisfying mixture of guilt and helplessness on the part of those who might otherwise lend assistance.

This, too, goes a long way toward explaining why more people do not help, but it does not justify this lack of assistance. It no more justifies it than if the passerby in the scenario above simply permitted the child to drown, reasoning that, even as this child was saved, other children would be suffering in innumerable ways. Indeed, why bother saving even this child when she may later fall into another pond, or be struck by an automobile, or develop a horrible illness? It is true, the *psychology* of the two situations is very different; the drowning child is perceived as one helpless individual while the starving child is yet another reminder of a huge problem that cannot be remedied in one fell swoop. But a refusal to act is not only morally unjustified, it becomes a self-fulfilling prophecy. The larger the problem, the less likely people are to want to act, and the less likely they are to act, the larger the problem may become.

On both a utilitarian and a deontological approach, a strong case can be made for our obligation to help the starving in the Third World. The case is perhaps strongest on a utilitarian account. The more altruistic implications of the happiness- maximizing aspects of utilitarian theory have sometimes been the subject of criticism, some thinkers claiming that utilitarianism requires *too much* of people. Utilitarianism *requires* people to be altruistic in situations where most versions of deontological thought are relatively weaker. In fact, utilitarian theory entails what appear, from the standpoint of most forms of deontological thought, to be radical conclusions.

For example, few, if any, deontologists would claim that a person has a *duty* to sacrifice himself to save the lives of two other, similarly situated, persons. It is heroic if the one person should do so, but it certainly is not *morally required.* The utilitarian, on the other hand, appears to be in the position of having to argue that, far from heroic, such self-sacrifice is morally obligatory: if the happiness inherent in two lives can be preserved only by the sacrifice of yet a third life, then utilitarianism, with certain loopholes, requires just such a sacrifice of the agent. (Thus, those, like Rifkin, who associate utilitarianism with self-ishness, wastefulness, and mechanization are incorrect, in this respect, about the implications of utilitarian theory.)

The case at hand provides perhaps the best example. Here, the true utilitarian would argue that if we can feed the starving millions by relinquishing certain conveniences of our own, we are morally obligated to do so. If we must give up our snacks, our tobacco, our alcohol—or, indeed, as we shall shortly see, our meats—in order to save others from certain death, then we *must* do so. More happiness is to be gained, on the whole, by the malnourished child eating her first meal in days than by the well-fed child consuming another candy bar, for example. And when the prospect of the death of the starving child is factored into the equation, the utilitarian case for assistance becomes air-tight.

Similarly, from a deontological standpoint, to the extent that we have an obligation to save the drowning child in the scenario above, we also have a duty to intervene on behalf of the starving, particularly where doing so puts us at no great disadvantage. Of course, opponents may seek a way out by claiming that the passerby in the scenario has no moral duty to save the child (though, again, it would be praiseworthy if he did so). But the very obnoxiousness of this conclusion, the implications of which are that no moral wrong has been done if the witness simply walks on past the calling child, serves as the best retort to the claim that no moral duty exists.

Next, we must consider the "practical" objection, mentioned earlier, to feeding the malnourished of the world. This objection holds that hunger, famine, and chronic malnutrition are the results of overpopulation. As Malthus might have predicted at the end of the eighteenth century, the ever-escalating population of the Third World has outstripped increases in local food production. Hunger, famine, disease, and death are nature's way, the argument runs, of limiting population in conformity with available food supply. Feeding these people will result in even greater population increases and skyrocketing demands for food shortly down the line. At some point, the world will no longer be able to support all the hungry. When this point has been reached, the surplus population will die, the misery multiplied many times over. In bleak Darwinian terms the argument concludes that it is better to let natural selection take its course now, when it is still only a few hundred million, rather than a few billion, who are affected.

Estimates as to the number of human beings who could be supported by the earth's agricultural capacities vary greatly. At the optimistic end, Russian researchers have claimed that the earth can support as many as ten times what it now does, though this estimate depends upon not only a variety of radical agricultural reforms, but also upon the development of a number of high-tech, sci-fi nutrient factories. More moderately, others argue that, with appropriate agricultural reform and redistribution of resources, the earth could provide for up to twelve-and-a-half billion, two-and-a-half times the present population.[19] This, of course, does not mean that such a number is desirable, only that it could be done. Thus, the Malthusian cutoff line (the point to which we could provide for the needs of an expanding population) is still a long way away. Many lives can be saved in the meantime.

More importantly, however, we must understand the causes of overpopulation. Why is it that those with the least capacity to provide for their own appear to be multiplying at the fastest rate? While sheer ignorance of the uses of contraception undoubtedly plays a role in the explanation—and this problem is remediable, as modern China makes clear—another explanation is that the poorest have nothing to invest in but the next generation. In the developing countries, increasing the number of children one has best serves to increase the likelihood that one would be provided for in old age, a kind of Third World social security.[20] In this neo-Malthusian twist, a present response to poverty has even more pernicious long-term effects, creating even greater poverty in the end.

The response to overpopulation and world hunger is not to ignore them, hoping they will breed themselves out of existence. Natural selection may make for an accurate evolutionary *description* of the war of the species, but no law of science requires that it become the touchstone for all social engineering. The appropriate response to the problem of overpopulation is mass education of those in the Third World, along with an eradication of the poverty that fosters it.

We have spoken at some length in the past few pages of famine and overpopulation. How might widescale adoption of a vegetarian diet pose an answer to the problem of world hunger?

Meat Eating and World Hunger: The Argument for Vegetarianism

Today in the United States, over 70 percent of the grain produced is fed to cattle and various other livestock. Worldwide about a third of all grain is similarly disposed of.[21] Fully one-half of our total agricultural output each year in the United States goes to feed livestock.[22] This represents a tremendous investment in livestock—and an even more remarkable disinvestment in people, here and abroad.

In the United States and Canada, cereal-grain consumption per person is more than five times higher than in the developing countries. It is not that Americans eat more than five times as much cereal as those in the Third World. Indeed, we eat comparatively little grain directly. Rather, we consume these products indirectly through the meat we eat.[23] Nor is this to suggest that the secondhand human consumers of plant food actually derive the total nutritional benefit from the various grains and other products consumed by livestock. In reality, comparatively little nutritional value is derived. The reprocessing of food, from plant to animal to human, is an extremely wasteful process. Eating further up on the food chain entails the waste of the great majority of nutrients consumed at the lower end of the chain.

For example, it takes sixteen pounds of grain, soy, or other cereal product to produce one pound of beef. This sixteen pounds of grain produce contains twenty-one times the calories, eight times the protein, no fat, and a great deal more fiber than the same one pound of beef.[24] Most of the nutritive qualities of the cereal products are lost in "processing" through the animals that eat them. Only 11 percent of the feed produces beef. The remaining 89 percent is lost in the conversion process; it is either burned off by the animal in the process of living and maintaining bodily functions or goes into nonedible portions of the animal such as bones, teeth, and hair. Every 750 grams of plant protein consumed by cattle and livestock get whittled down to only 50 grams by the time the animal is eaten.[25] The amount of grain and soy lost in the conversion process *in the United States alone* each year is equal to one cup of grain per day every day for every human on earth.[26] This same amount of grain, if converted into monetary form, would be worth approximately twenty billion dollars.[27]

The same relationship can be seen from the standpoint of the amount of land necessary to yield a certain amount of protein. One thousand acres of rice, soybeans, corn, or wheat each yield, with some variation between them, roughly one thousand pounds of usable protein, about a pound of protein per acre of land. When this same amount of plant food is served up to livestock, only 125 pounds of usable protein remain.[28] Seven-eighths of the protein has been used up in the process of conversion.

In chapter 3 we saw that there is absolutely no truth to the claim that "animal protein" is superior in quality to "plant protein." All protein *is* plant protein in the sense that no animal produces protein; all protein comes from plants. Thus, there is no advantage, from a nutritional standpoint, in eating animals, rather than plant food. As we also saw in chapter 3, there are plenty of disadvantages, from the standpoint of health, in doing so.

In addition to the waste of the earth's nutritional resources inherent in feeding half of our agricultural output to animals, livestock production negatively affects our ability to produce more food in a second way as well. A great portion of the land that could be put to the production of grains and other nutrient-rich plantfood is put to use instead as pastureland for livestock. There are today about one billion cattle on the earth. This is in addition to sheep, hogs, and other farm animals, which undoubtedly number in excess of one billion. *Remarkably, one-quarter of the total surface land area of the planet is utilized for livestock grazing. In the United States, the figure is even higher: 29 percent of the total landmass of the United States is used as grazing land.*[29] Most importantly, most of this land is arable and could be put to numerous other agricultural purposes.

To sum up, food that could save the starving millions around the globe is lost to them in three ways. First, grain that could go directly to the mouths of starving people goes instead to feed farm animals. As much as 90 percent of the protein and other nutrients in plants is lost in the conversion process. Second, land that could be put to the use of further agricultural production is instead used for grazing. Crops that would otherwise be grown and could make up the food deficit in the world are in fact never grown. Thus, between the lost nutritional resources of the plant food we *do* grow and the lost resources of the plant food we do *not* grow (to permit livestock grazing), we produce as a nation only a tiny fraction of what we could produce in terms of nutritional value.

Finally, a result of these two conditions, the more limited

supply of grain in the world drives grain prices higher than what they would otherwise be. The poorest in the world are unable to afford the higher priced grain and must go without. Of course, the situation is only further exacerbated by government subsidies paid to farmers to induce them not to grow these products, a policy directly aimed at keeping grain prices inflated.

If proponents of the argument for vegetarianism are correct, then the misery endured by as many as a billion other human beings worldwide could be easily allayed by even a relatively small reduction in meat eating (or an increase in surplus grain production). The scenario, however, is rather more complicated than some of these advocates suggest. The reason for this is that one other assumption has been left unmentioned—an assumption that is, in fact, untrue. The false assumption is that there is now a deficit in the food supply worldwide.

Advocates of the argument for vegetarianism are correct that a transition to vegetarianism will have a salutary effect on the problem of world hunger, but not entirely for the reasons they suggest. Before discussing the way in which widescale adoption of vegetarianism will greatly ameliorate world hunger, we must briefly discuss the true causes of hunger and famine.

The Causes of World Hunger

Perhaps the greatest myth concerning world hunger is that it is precipitated entirely by a shortage of food worldwide. Experts are (uncommonly) in agreement that there is presently enough food to feed everyone in the world. A report for the Independent Commission on International Humanitarian Issues states that "[t]he world has enough to eat. The difficulty is that nations and individuals often lack the money to purchase it."[30] The report cites the World Bank Development Project, which maintains: "The main issue is not the worldwide availability of food, but the capacity of nations, groups within nations and individuals to obtain enough food for a healthy diet."[31] This view is confirmed by numerous other experts, including Lappé and Collins, who write that "[a]bundance, not scarcity, best describes the supply of food in the world today."[32]

The problem is not with production but with the distribution of food. As Arthur Simon, the executive director for Bread for the World wrote in the mid-1970s:

> If present world food production were evenly divided among all the world's people, with minimal waste, everyone would have enough. Barely enough, perhaps, but enough. However, the world's food supply is not evenly divided. The rich fourth produce and consume more than half of the world's grain. The other three-fourths produce and consume less than half. . . . To adequately nourish everyone with present levels of production would take a near-utopian arrangement, and even that would not insure enough food for tomorrow. [33]

By the most recent estimates, the food needed to feed the one billion who either lack enough to eat or are at risk of starvation is very tiny. Around 750 million could be fed with only two percent of the world's grain harvest, an amount equivalent to slightly more than 10 percent of the *unsold* wheat and rice stocks.[34]

Thus, starvation is as much a manmade economic disaster as it is the product of meteorological and geographical factors. The causes of chronic hunger include the political and economic legacy of colonialism: countries with one-crop economies (itself a postcolonial hangover of colonial economic policies) may be devastated by the vicissitudes of natural conditions such as drought or crop blight or by the fluctuation of economic factors that may send market prices for the crop plummeting. Burdened by smaller loan inflows, higher interest payments, and an increasing national debt, Third World nations may lack the funds to pay workers or to buy the necessary parts for farm machinery; similarly, they may rely upon the production of crops that generate the most export dollars, rather than those that feed the indigenous population. These and other economic conditions have fostered widespread hunger and, in its more virulent manifestation, famine.[35]

A variety of political factors, both internal and international, also affect food production and distribution in the Third World. For example, government policies in many African and Asian nations favor urban dwellers by placing price limits on produce, thereby burdening the rural native farmer. More significantly, intermittent warfare limits both the available funds to combat famine and the ability of foreign aid agencies to assist in the short term. In the 1980s, Ethiopia, Chad, Angola, Sudan, and Mozambique were all torn by civil war. All were also among the hardest-hit countries by the famine of the 1980s.

Finally, and perhaps ironically, even international aid in too great a quantity can have pernicious long-term effects on the economy by depressing local crop prices and discouraging farmers from growing such crops. This simply precipitates local food shortages the following year.

In addition to the spectrum of political and economic factors, there are the effects of nature, typically abetted in its destructiveness by wasteful and short-sighted environmental policies. The African drought of the 1980s greatly aggravated the rampant deforestation and desertification that had taken place as the result of livestock production and other agricultural practices endemic in large areas of the Third World. As a result both of the drought and these other practices, today the Sahara desert is advancing at a rate of 3.7 million acres a year, and advance on the front line of about six kilometers (almost four miles) a year.[36] These conditions, of course, most directly limit the ability of the poorer countries to provide for their own by consuming forever the cropland that might feed the starving.

The causes of world hunger, then, are many and varied. Hunger is largely the result of mismanagement and wastefulness; minimally, it could be greatly prevented or ameliorated by a combination of prescient policies and international openheartedness. Thus, the argument for vegetarianism, as it has been presented by some writers, has greatly oversimplified the causes of world hunger. It also, however, has tended to oversimplify the solutions.

In two respects, the argument for vegetarianism as it is usually made has neglected two other important considerations, one short-term and one long-term. The argument proceeds from the true premise that meat eating is an extremely wasteful practice, nutritionally, and from the standpoint of the most efficient use for our resources, and concludes that vegetarianism is the best response to world hunger. Because we in the First World would have more grain and other produce if vegetarianism were more popular, there would be more to give away. The argument assumes that the cure to world hunger is to place the First World, more or less permanently, in the position of provider for the Third World's food needs. But this is a highly unsatisfactory response for two reasons.

As a short-term matter, having adequate resources here in the developed countries does not automatically entail that we will be able to get these resources to where they are needed. Bulk food shipments can take up to four months to reach their destination, from the time of the report of the need to the time the food is received.[37] This, of course, may be too late for those on the edge of starvation. Moreover, there are numerous logistical obstacles to delivery of such food. Ports may have only a limited capacity to handle shipments. (In some African ports, the harbors are so narrow that ships must line up, one at a time, to await unloading.) Inadequate roads and other necessary infrastructure frequently prevent delivery of the food to the (often rural) areas where it is needed most. Finally, as with the Ethiopian civil war, the prospect of war may make delivery difficult or impossible. All of these factors limit our ability, as a practical matter, to respond to the need, notwithstanding early warning systems of various sorts.

Second, as a long-term matter, the obligation of the First World is not to perpetuate this dependent donor-donee relationship, but to assist the poorer countries in becoming self-sufficient. Short-term aid is necessary to combat the immediate problem of famine, but unless the Third World is to remain forever dependent upon the First, the long-term policy must be to assist the developing world to create its own reliable agricultural system.[38] Thus, to the extent the argument for vegetarianism implies that present world hunger is the result of a worldwide shortage of food, it is misleading; moreover, to the extent it implies that the primary obligation of the wealthy countries should be to feed the rest of the world without assisting them in feeding themselves, it is simply bad policy.

Given the great complexity of causes and solutions for the problem of world hunger, how would adoption of the vegetarian diet help the fight against world hunger in the short- and the long-term? It is to this question that we now turn.

Would Universal Vegetarianism
Cure World Hunger?

What would be the overall economic effect of adoption of a vegetarian diet, either here or abroad? Ironically, as vegetarianism
becomes more popular, there will be a *significant decrease* in
demand for grains, cereals, and other such vegetable products.
This, as we have seen, is because the amount of vegetable products needed to feed people directly is much smaller than the
amount of vegetable products necessary to feed animals that are
then eaten by people.

Again, ironically, on the supply side of the equation, an increase in the number of vegetarians would lead, at least initially,
to an *increased* supply of vegetable products as commodities that
were formerly fed to cattle and other livestock are no longer
needed. Also, because vast areas of arable land formerly used
for grazing could be put to use to grow still more grain, wheat,
soybeans, corn, or other products, our capacity to produce plant
food would be significantly augmented. The combined result of
the decreased demand for, and the increased supply of, vegetable products would be that prices for these products would plum-
met, making them more affordable.

Of course, the market would adjust to these changes to some
extent. Some grain growers, unable to compete, would go out of
business. Others would find more profitable uses for their land.
This would have a leveling effect, curtailing some of the supply.
Also, the government could always step in, restricting supply and
artificially inflating prices as it now does by paying some farmers to leave their land fallow. Similarly, some of these commodities might be stored for sale at a later date, as happens now.
Even this, however, is a short-term maneuver that would only
forestall the fall in prices. Thus, notwithstanding these market
adjustments, a widescale move to vegetarianism here or abroad
would result overall in significantly lower grain prices. This
would make the purchase of rice, wheat, soybeans, corn, barley,
and other staples by the poorest of the poor (nations and individuals) much easier, staving off starvation for perhaps hundreds
of millions.

A movement to a vegetarian diet in the First World would

have yet another ameliorative effect on hunger in the Third World. A great deal of agriculture in the developing world is put to raising animals for export to the United States and other developed countries. In Central and South America, particularly Costa Rica, Columbia, Brazil, and Argentina, livestock production takes up immense tracts of land.[39] In East Africa, *over 50 percent* of the land area is utilized for cattle production.[40] Much of the area is coextensive with the areas hardest hit by desertification and famine in the 1980s. As land that could be put to use for production of plant food is used instead for grazing, millions go hungry. As cereal products that could go to feed the hungry are instead fed to cattle and other livestock, millions starve to death each year. Thus, the resources of the Third World are often put to use in producing cheap First World meat while millions in these same countries suffer the lingering effects of malnutrition. Without a market for meat in the developed countries, indigenous farmers will turn back to the production of cereal products that, again, will sell at prices much lower than present levels.

But the problem with the worldwide production of meat for the First World goes even deeper than this. As we saw in chapter 4, livestock production is directly related to the deforestation and desertification of large areas of the planet. Not surprisingly, desert frequently sits where livestock formerly grazed. And once arable land becomes desert—once the necessary topsoil for agriculture is lost—it is lost, for our purposes, forever. Put simply, as livestock production continues, the problem of famine and starvation is only going to get worse in these areas of the globe.

In short, a move to vegetarianism in the First World would not only lead to lower grain prices on a worldwide basis, it would also mean an end to the use of the Third World as giant feedlots for the First World, thereby returning the land to those who need it most—the hungry living in these countries. (Incidentally, worldwide livestock production historically has brought about great waves of displacement of peasants from their land. An end to the production of meat could also portend an end to the perennial disenfranchisement of indigenous peoples by cattle ranchers and livestock raisers.)

There is, however, yet a fourth way in which a move to vegetarianism here and abroad would ameliorate the problem of world hunger and famine. It is more indirect, perhaps more abstract, and unquestionably more difficult to articulate than the economic effects just discussed. Yet it is every bit as palpable in its significance for the plight of one billion fellow human beings who regularly do not have enough to eat.

The last factor has to do with the psychological—dare we even say, the *moral*—effects of a vegetarian diet upon those who have relinquished meat. It is not clear whether a concern for the environment, for one's health, and for the health and well-being of others leads one to become a vegetarian or whether becoming a vegetarian positively fosters these more altruistic inclinations, but, most likely, a bit of both is true. I know of no study that has been conducted on the question, but anecdotal experience strongly suggests that, as some people become vegetarians, they develop a kind of moral empowerment—a greatly expanded sense of individual responsibility and a commitment to a variety of issues outside their own skin. With surprising regularity, vegetarians report such a change in their own psychological outlook after they made the transition to a meatless diet.

This empowerment may be the consequence of any of a number of different factors, or perhaps a combination thereof. It may result from an increased sense of the indirect consequences of one's actions upon the world. Or perhaps it is the result of knowing that one has already taken a stand and made a decision on an important issue—and can do the same again on another issue if necessary. Or perhaps, as some suggest, there is actually a psychophysiological effect, a change in one's psychological and moral temperament brought about by the elimination of meat from the diet. This certainly poses a fascinating possibility—imagine changing the world by changing its diet—and there are many who argue that such an effect is real. (See chapter 3 for a discussion of this.) What is striking is that, on the whole, vegetarians do appear to be more committed, more "tuned in" to issues affecting others—both people and animals—around the planet.

Widespread vegetarianism in the First World or, better yet, around the globe (much of the population in the Third World is already largely *de facto* vegetarian, by economic circumstance if not by choice) would effect a transformed social and political environment worldwide. This is not a panacea nor is the claim being made that utopia awaits just around the corner. Rather, the moral empowerment of large members of the world population means a better world, a more committed world, a less apathetic, alienated, and self-destructive world. Widespread or universal vegetarianism may mean a world where hunger has been checked, if not forever banished.

To sum up, adoption of a vegetarian diet on a widescale basis will lead to lower grain prices for the poor of the world. Further, as the market in meat dried up, Third World countries would return to the production of plant food, a greater percentage of which would be used to feed the hungry at home. Finally, the more indirect, psychological effects of vegetarianism could have their results in a variety of ways on the problem of the maldistribution of food in the world, and upon the maldistribution of wealth, which underlies this and many other social problems.

If adoption of a vegetarian diet can have even some of these beneficial effects, there can be no doubt what must be done. If even a small percentage of the one billion human beings who now endure hunger, a smaller number suffering famine, and a smaller but still significant number (forty to sixty million) who die annually at the hands of hunger and hunger-related illness could be spared their fate by our individual and collective willingness to relinquish our taste for animal flesh, we must do so. Only sheer moral blindness or the obstinacy and fear that come with living well at the expense of others could counsel a contrary decision.

Most essentially, one need not be an advocate of animal rights in order to see the fundamental importance of vegetarianism. Commitment to human rights is alone sufficient.

Chapter Six

Some Objections to Vegetarianism Considered

In the previous chapters, we have discussed the case for vegetarianism. It is now time to turn to a number of objections that are made to vegetarianism. This chapter should prove particularly entertaining for two reasons. First, a number of the objections that will be considered here constitute classic examples of certain forms of informal logical fallacies. Not only will the reader be armed with responses to the objections as they arise in the context of the debate over vegetarianism but, since these kinds of fallacies occur in a variety of contexts, this chapter will be helpful in learning how to counter certain rhetorical moves generally, whether the debate be over vegetarianism, affirmative action, abortion, or other topics.

Second, familiarity with some of these objections makes it clear the extent to which people will go to avoid a conclusion they find uncomfortable. A good friend of mine (who still eats meat) regularly engages me in argument when we find ourselves together in a restaurant. (He is, like me, a lawyer; he also prides himself on what he perceives to be his rhetorical abilities.) It will start with my asking the server at a restaurant about some selection on the menu. My friend will interject, saying something like, "He's a vegetarian. Maybe you have a ball of lettuce you can throw his way." From there, the debate escalates, culminating in a series of what are often lame objections to vegetarianism. This chapter is dedicated to him and to the friends of vegetarians everywhere who (at least for now) continue to eat animals.

149

The Argument from Nonexistence, or
"I Eat Animals So That They May
Live in the First Place"

One of the most interesting objections raised by nonvegetarians purports to argue, as if from the standpoint of animals themselves, that meat eating is actually good for animals. It is good because, if we did not eat meat, many animals would not be born at all. In other words, to the extent cows, chickens, hogs, and other animals are bred and raised to be eaten, they owe their very existence to the carnivorous habits of humans.

This objection has been made by a number of writers. James Cargile writes:

> Every year I buy several pigs from a neighboring hog farm and raise them to slaughter for food. They are given lots of room and food, everything a pig could want for a good life—but a short one. It would be nice if they could have longer lives. But I believe that their good, short life is better than no life at all. Thus, I think I have done more for the happiness of pigs than most vegetarians.[1]

Similarly, Jan Narveson, a moral philosopher, writes that "[i]n current circumstances, it is certainly true that there would be very few domestic animals if vegetarianism held sway, and so it is true that . . . [t]he cow is doing a lot better with slaughter than it would without."[2]

Another author scales the very peak of irony when he puts similar sentiments into the mouth of a two-year-old Hereford steer: "I wish you vegetarians would not work so hard trying to discourage people from eating meat. Because if you succeed, I and my kind will cease to exist."[3]

In order to analyze this objection, we will place it in standard syllogistic form, that is, with premises and a conclusion. The Argument from Nonexistence appears to take the following form:

Premise One: Existence is always preferable to Nonexistence.

Premise Two: If vegetarianism were to become widely accepted fewer (farm) animals would exist.

Conclusion: Thus, even from the standpoint of the farm animal, meat eating is preferable to vegetarianism.

There are a number of amusing things to note about this type of objection. First, its proponent purports to be doing animals a *favor* by raising them to eat. But, of course, the meat eater is not doing the animal anything of the sort; rather, he is rationalizing his behavior. The man who buys pigs to raise and kill is not motivated by anything remotely approaching good will toward the animals he slaughters. The meat eater is motivated by one thing and one thing only: his own taste for animal flesh. Thus, at best, even if the objection had some truth—even if animals were, in general, better with meat eating than without—it would be a mere fortuitous coincidence from the standpoint of the meat eater. The hog farmer would be eating meat even if it were not in the best interest of his animals. This is why this objection is pure rationalization.

More significantly, however, the objection is shot through with logical and moral difficulties. The problem with the Argument from Nonexistence is that all manner of strange implications appear to follow from it. For example, if existence in whatever form and under whatever conditions really were always preferable to nonexistence, it would be completely morally permissible for any person to bring any other person into this world for the purpose of enslaving her. Imagine a ring of vicious physicians who buy human sperm and ova from sperm and ova banks. Through the process of *in vitro* fertilization (the test-tube baby process), they create a number of fertilized ova which they then give to surrogate mothers to gestate to full term. Upon birth, the surrogate mothers exchange the newborn babies for a fee. The physicians then raise these children on a private island for a variety of nefarious purposes.

As with chickens, our physician-entrepreneurs might destroy the male newborns immediately or raise them to a tender age and then slaughter them for their flesh. As for the female babies, they are to be raised as "breeders," just as female chickens are. This dark scenario proceeds as the girls are raised to be sex slaves for wealthy patrons willing to pay exorbitant prices for these girls and young women. Finally, at about age twenty-five, after they have borne still other children to continue the next generation of this modest experiment, these young women are "sacrificed." And it can all be justified with similar reasoning as

that of the Argument from Nonexistence. After all, existence is
always preferable to nonexistence and these children would not
have been born at all were it not for the beneficence of this
medical crew in bringing them into this world.

This sci-fi example in response to the Argument from Nonexistence serves to show that we may never bring a being into the
world for the purpose of violating its rights.[4] The meat eater may
contend that this response goes for people but not for animals.
Of course, they might reason, it would be morally abhorrent to
bring people into the world for the purpose of enslaving them.
But animals are a different matter. Human life is sacred, the argument might conclude, but not so with animal life.

The response to this counterobjection takes us back to issues
of animal rights discussed in chapter 2. Most basically, why
should only human life be viewed as sacred? From a deontological standpoint, animals are sentient creatures whose existence is a positive good to them. Superior intelligence gives
human beings no more right to kill animals than it would be-
stow upon some superintelligent extraterrestrial the right to eat
humans.

Yet another response to the Argument from Nonexistence is
that it is simply not true that existence under any circumstances
is preferable to nonexistence. There is a point at which any existence can become so burdened, so painful, or so devoid of hope
or meaning that nonexistence might indeed be the rational alternative. This becomes all too evident if we place ourselves in the
position of animals on the factory farms. If given the choice,
how many people would choose the short life of the veal calf to
never having been born at all? How many would find the prospect of confinement in a pen not much larger than the size of
our bodies, to be prevented from making any movements that
might facilitate the development of muscles so that we were
forced to crouch or lie down, without even the possibility of
turning around in our pen? Who would gladly accept the unappetizing gruel designed to keep us half alive long enough for us
to reach the age where we will then be slaughtered unceremoniously, within sight of other similarly condemned creatures, but
not before we have witnessed the fate of those ahead of us and
have recoiled at the prospect of our own imminent slaughter?

Who would willingly countenance the eventuality of castration, or the human equivalent of debeaking, forced molting, branding, or any of the other similar injuries and indignities that are to be the lot of animals on the factory farm? In contemplating these very real facts about the existence of most farm animals, we must admit that we do these animals no favor by bringing them into this world.

There is, finally, yet another response to the Argument from Nonexistence. The argument assumes that, were vegetarianism to be universally accepted, many forms of animal life would simply cease to exist. Since we are no longer eating animals in such large quantities, the argument maintains, such animals will not be born at all. But while certain forms of farm animals would certainly exist in much smaller numbers if vegetarianism were to become the norm, remember that a reduction in meat eating would free up as much as 90 percent of land formerly used for crops and grazing.[5] While cows and pigs would be less plentiful, there would be newfound space for other animals including deer and other prairie animals. Thus, a loss to certain species would be a gain to others.

To sum up, the Argument from Nonexistence does little to advance the case for meat eating. First, Premise One is false. Existence is not always preferable to nonexistence. We are not the beneficent beings the argument implies by virtue of the fact that we bring the farm animal into existence only to maim, confine, exploit, and then slaughter it. Nor does our role in bringing an animal into the world give us a right to do with it as we choose. Second, Premise Two is true only if limited to *farm* animals. Widespread acceptance of vegetarianism would result in a reduction in the number of farm animals. But it would also lead to a dramatic increase in the number of other species of animals as crop and grazing land is freed up. And these animals would not have to live under the horrible conditions endemic in the meat and dairy industries today. Finally, in addition to the problems with the argument itself, there is something more than a bit disingenuous about meat eaters defending their right to consume the flesh of other animals on the ground that the animals would themselves *really prefer it*. Thus, the Argument from Nonexistence must be rejected.

The Argument from Inconvenience

The Argument from Inconvenience is not much in the way of an argument at all; it is rather, at best, the result of a lack of knowledge and, at worst, an expression of indifference or moral inertia. The argument moves from the premise that being a vegetarian is difficult or inconvenient to the conclusion (to the extent there is a conscious conclusion drawn at all) that the person should not or need not become a vegetarian. Though this objection is of little interest logically, it is probably the most important reason, as a practical matter, that many people do not become vegetarians. The fear is that becoming a vegetarian will be difficult or that maintaining the diet will be burdensome, socially and otherwise.

What can be said by way of response to this concern? First, of course, as a moral matter, it does not follow from the fact that a particular act or form of behavior is inconvenient that one has no obligation to pursue it. It was inconvenient for Southern slaveholders to give up slavery, but this was no argument in defense of slaveholding. Similarly, the contention that meat eating is easier, more pleasurable, or more convenient is no defense to the practice of killing animals for food. Thus, the Argument from Inconvenience is logically invalid—that is, the conclusion that vegetarianism is not a sound idea does not follow from the premise that vegetarianism is inconvenient. More to the point, however, the argument's single premise is simply not true. Vegetarianism is not inconvenient at all.

As a matter of strategy, of course, it does not suit the vegetarian's case to tell an audience of meat eaters that inconvenience is no excuse. (It *isn't*, but it usually does little good to say so.) Responses such as this on the part of the vegetarian will often have, or will be viewed to have, the distinct flavor of sanctimonious condescension; further, while the response carries logical force, it carries precious little psychological force. In short, people seldom care that their actions are not predicated upon sound logic.

The better strategy is to understand that this objection comes from a concern on the part of the nonvegetarian regarding the social consequences of becoming a vegetarian. The meat eater has a right to be concerned about whether adopting a vegetarian diet will adversely affect her lifestyle. Here, it is facts and not logic to which the vegetarian must appeal.

First, becoming a vegetarian is not difficult at all. A recent survey indicates that only 27 percent of lacto-ovo vegetarians— vegetarians who consume cheese, eggs, milk and other dairy products, but who eat no animal meat—found giving up meat difficult.[6] It appears to be more difficult for some to go from meat eating or lacto-ovo vegetarianism to veganism—vegans eat no eggs or dairy products and live purely on vegetable products— than from meat eating to lacto-ovo vegetarianism. (This is due in part to the fact that eggs, butter, cheese, milk, and cream are used in a wide variety of baked goods and commercial foods.) Moreover, even for those who experience some difficulty in the initial transition to vegetarianism, the new diet becomes second nature in a short period of time.

Where the transition to vegetarianism is difficult, it often has more to do with habits, than with the taste for meat. The new vegetarian must learn to negotiate restaurants, supermarkets, barbecues, and outings within the parameters of her new diet. Once one knows which groceries to buy, which restaurants have the best nonmeat selections, what to eat at barbecues, and so on, the problem of inconvenience disappears. Increasingly in all geographical areas throughout the nation, the call to reduce meat in the diet has been met by grocers and restaurateurs with a surprisingly varied array of dishes. Particularly over the course of the last five to ten years, the widespread availability of vegetarian burgers and franks, "wheat meats," tofu dishes, pastas, and similar products has made vegetarian cooking easy. Today, the vegetarian diet is easily achieved without sacrificing social mobility. One need not become a hermit, a recluse, or a social outcast to relinquish meat eating.

Not only is the conversion to vegetarianism easy for most, but the benefits one immediately derives from the diet (see chapter 3) also provides the new vegetarian with the natural impetus to forge ahead with the new lifestyle. In my own experience, the switch to lacto-ovo vegetarianism was about as easy, natural, and immediately rewarding as anything I have ever done.

Nor is maintaining a vegetarian diet difficult. After mastering one's culinary options as a vegetarian, perhaps the next greatest concern is the social consequences of observing a vegetarian diet: How will others respond to this still infrequent dietary predilection? When I was fresh out of law school, I began working at a large Chicago banking law firm. At first, interview dinners and firm functions were an invitation to stealth vegetarianism. Silk stocking lawyers, after all, did not go in for such "fads" or moral "self-indulgence" on the part of their new associates.[7] Consequently, I would quietly order pastas and salads and no one was the wiser.

Finally, however, I grew tired of this culinary subterfuge and "came out of the closet," so to speak. My aim was not to proselytize, but simply to be open and at ease with my diet, and with the convictions that underwrote it. The response was, with one exception, either neutral or very positive. Those who were health conscious loved the idea; others admired my position for a variety of moral and ecological reasons. A few people even remarked that my consistency in maintaining the diet was a mark of "good moral character." (Little did they know how easy—even self-perpetuating—the vegetarian diet is.)

What about the one exception? This leads us to another aspect of the claim that vegetarianism is inconvenient: How should the vegetarian respond to the vulgarian who wishes to ridicule vegetarianism or pick a fight? In the case at hand, I was attending a law firm dinner. When I asked the waitress for the vegetarian plate I had ordered in advance, another recent associate sitting at the same table started in, "What? A vegetarian? We have a vegetarian here," etc, etc. When he persisted, I asked him exactly what his objection was. (In argument, as in warfare, it is always easier to defend than to attack. Most of the time, you will find that your interlocutor really does not have a coherent objection. This was the case here.) As it turned out, my inquisitor was the son of a butcher. It was nothing but prejudice, and perhaps some loyalty to his father, that animated the attack. The following day he apologized for the remarks.

In general, experience has shown me that the best way to handle such situations is simply to let the offending party indict himself, either by his ignorance, his prejudice or the sheer silliness of the attack. Anger and condescension are not warranted.

Usually, the vegetarian will find that even where others do not share her dietary choice, they will defend her right to make that choice; thus, the offending party will be immediately ostracized. The best response is to place the burden on the other party, and to (very nicely) obliterate his position with facts and arguments elaborated here and elsewhere.

A final interesting aspect of the Argument from Inconvenience is that it is a self-perpetuating myth. The more people accept the argument and abjure vegetarianism, the more inconvenient vegetarianism will be for those who choose it. Conversely, the more widespread vegetarianism becomes, the more the market will respond with vegetarian alternatives to meat dishes. Similarly, the more popular vegetarianism becomes—and every indication is that vegetarianism is on a permanent cultural upswing—the wider its social acceptance, which, in turn, positively affects its popularity as a lifestyle choice.

The Argument from Innate Human Aggression and the "Naturalness" of Killing

In chapter 3, we examined the claim that humans are "natural" carnivores. We saw that the contention that eating meat is morally permissible because our ancestors did it suffers from a number of the same logical flaws that befall natural-law arguments generally. In essence, what we mean by "natural" can be a slippery notion. Even if we could establish that some behavior were indeed natural, it would not follow logically that such behavior is morally proper or even obligatory. Murder may well be perfectly natural in some sense of the word and yet it would remain a moral abomination from the modern moral standpoint.

The present objection takes two slightly varying forms. The first strain of the argument resembles a natural-law argument. It provides that human beings are "innately aggressive" and that killing is a natural component of human behavior. It would be "unnatural," the argument continues, to become vegetarians because we have always been and, presumably, will always be, violent creatures. Thus, the argument differs from the natural-law argument examined in chapter 3 in that this argument concludes not that meat-eating is physiologically required by our evolutionary past, but that vegetarianism is inconsistent with our psychological makeup.

Certainly there is ample anthropological evidence of our rapacious biological heritage. Raymond Dart, the discoverer of *Australopithecus*, the earliest hominoid from which *Homo sapiens* is descended, wrote in 1953:

> The blood bespattered, slaughter gutted archives of human history from the evident Egyptian and Sumerian records to the most recent atrocities of the Second World War accord with early universal cannibalism, with animal and human sacrificial practices or their substitutes in formalized religions, and with the worldwide scalping, head-hunting, body mutilating and necrophilic practices of mankind in proclaiming this common bloodlust differentiator, this predaceous habit, this mark of Cain that separates man dietetically from his anthropoidal relatives and allies him rather with the deadliest of carnivores.[8]

Australopithecus, we now know, routinely cannibalized fellow *Australopithecines*. More recent evidence indicates that murder, infanticide, and cannibalism is found among wild chimpanzees, our closest subhominoid relative.[9] With such evolutionary precedent, the argument from innate human aggression may appear quite compelling.

The question as to whether human beings are innately aggressive has preoccupied and divided anthropologists and social scientists for over a century. Despite our biological precursors, however, and notwithstanding the more recent historical record, there is much to recommend the conclusion that, minimally, many of these claims have been overstated.

To begin with, there is as much evidence in the historical record to suggest that we are similarly sympathetic, empathetic, and even self-sacrificing creatures, as there is to support the contrary conclusion. Are we then also innately beneficent? And what does the claim of innate aggression amount to anyway? Is it to say that we are *inevitably* aggressive? Certainly this is not true. At most, the claim must amount to the notion that we are capable, if placed under unfavorable conditions, of aggressive or violent behavior. Presumably, if placed under better conditions, we would be similarly capable of the most altruistic behavior. Should we thus conclude that we are innately altruistic as well?

The controversy concerning innate human aggression has been explored recently elsewhere.[10] There are compelling reasons for accepting a brighter view of human nature. But, notwithstanding this controversy—and even if the assertion that we are "innately aggressive," whatever this might mean, turned out to be true—it would be irrelevant nevertheless. Again, it does not follow from the dubious proposition that we are, as human beings, innately aggressive that meat eating is somehow permissible or even obligatory any more than this same assertion excuses the murder of other human beings. Human beings make choices and they can make them for the better. To hold otherwise is to subscribe to the crassest form of biological determinism. The past may be prologue, but it does not necessarily and inevitably repeat itself.

The second strain of the objection from the naturalness of killing focuses not on innate aggression as a fundamental component of human nature, but on the fact that death is a part of life, and that killing is part of nature generally. What Darwin called "the warfare of nature" is similarly reflected in an ancient Buddhist poem:

> Looking deep he [the Buddha] saw
> The thorns which grow upon the rose of life . . .
> How lizard fed on ant and snake on him,
> And kite on both; and how the fishhawk robbed
> The fish-tiger of that which it had seized . . .
> Till everywhere each slew a slayer and in turn was slain
> Life living upon death. . . . So the fair one saw
> Veiled one vast, savage, grim conspiracy
> Of mutual murder, from the worm to man[11]

The second strain of the argument maintains, perhaps with sadness but also with a grim sense of practicality, simply that our preoccupation with death is unnatural. All things die, after all, and the vegetarian's abhorrence of this very natural process is almost pathological. The point is not that human beings must kill, as with the first strain of this objection, but that everything must die. As such, living off the flesh of animals is, once again, a natural part of existence itself. Thus, vegetarianism constitutes a refusal to accept this most basic law of nature.

There are a number of responses to be considered here. First, and perhaps most fundamentally, the fact that all things die as part of the natural process does not give humans a warrant to kill. In other contexts, philosophers have long observed the distinction between killing and letting die.[12] The distinction has received such consummate elaboration that conservative moral philosophers often argue that it would be wrong to hasten the death of the terminally ill patient who is in a great deal of pain—even if the patient requests it—precisely because this would constitute actively killing, rather than passively letting die. And whatever one feels about this conclusion in the context of the dying—even if one feels the wishes of the dying should be observed—surely there is a world of difference between hastening the death of a suffering, terminally ill patient at his own request and cutting short the life of innocent, often very young animals.

The fact that all things must die is not a warrant to kill. The conclusion might be different if our very survival depended upon eating the flesh of other animals. I argued in chapter 2 that human interests have priority over the interests of animals where it is strictly a matter of survival and where the cost in terms of animal lives is not great in comparison to the benefits to be gained by humans or other animals. This conclusion might justify certain forms of medical research, but there is no such necessity in the case of our dietary requirements. Indeed, as we established in chapter 3, humans are much better off, both physically and mentally, without meat.

The distinction between killing and letting die also serves to refute the objection, occasionally proffered by the nonvegetarian, that if animals have a right to life, as animal rights activists imply, we also have a duty to prevent predators from killing their prey. In short, the objection claims that our obligations require not simply that we *refrain* from killing, but that we *prevent* any killing of animals, even by other animals.

The fact that we have an obligation not to kill, however, does not mean that we have an obligation to intervene in the natural process. To put it another way, animals have a *negative* right not to be killed by humans, not a *positive* right to our intervention. Humans have a duty of nonmaleficence to animals—that is, a duty not to do harm—even if there is no corresponding duty of beneficence—that is, a duty to do positive good. This distinction, cast in law and moral philosophy variously as the distinction between a positive and a negative right, the duty of beneficence and the duty of nonmaleficence, or an act and an omission, is a fundamental tenet of our Western moral tradition. Thus, the vegetarian need not be the universal savior of all animals everywhere.

Finally, vegetarianism is not simply a response to the killing of animals; it is also a response to the way in which animals are exploited and abused at the hands of modern meat-processing facilities. Thus, the objection from the naturalness of killing misses the point, or at least one aspect of vegetarianism. Vegetarianism is an active and positive response to the great amount of unnecessary suffering of animals, whether this is the result of the way in which animals die, or the way in which they live at our hands.

Line-drawing Problems, or "Vegetarians Kill Plants, Don't They?"

If the injunction from Exodus, "Thou shalt not kill," is taken literally, vegetarians appear to be in the same hot water inhabited by their meat-eating friends. Nonvegetarians sometimes take the opportunity of using exactly this claim to argue that the vegetarian is as guilty as the meat eater. After all, even the vegetarian must kill to survive. As one writer put it, "If we do not kill animals, we must kill plants, for there is no alternative to consuming living things to fulfill our nutritional needs."[13] After defending the proposition that plants possess consciousness on grounds that no clear dividing line can be drawn between the conscious and the nonconscious, another author writes:

> One solution to the dilemma of eating is offered by fructarians who eat only fruit and seeds. But it is not clear that the destruction of seeds is less catastrophic than the destruction of more mature plants. The mature plant has had at least some life experience, while the potential life experience of the eaten seed is totally unfulfilled. The ingestion of any living or potentially living thing could be avoided by eating only milk and honey, but consuming milk requires that cows eat living things.[14]

There are two types of logical fallacies that often occur in debate and that make themselves particularly well known in the realm of moral debate. As such, the vegetarian often encounters each. The fallacies are closely related and are sometimes confused. The first is called the Sorites paradox, sometimes more informally called the "argument of the beard." The second is the "fallacy of black and white thinking." The Sorites paradox involves problems of line drawing and will be discussed in this section. The fallacy of black and white thinking occurs when its proponent attempts to require that the other party choose one of two extreme alternatives. It is also the result of a kind of inability to draw lines and take a practical position in the world. We will examine the fallacy of black and white thinking in the following section.

The Sorites paradox is the result of the inherent imprecision of our language. It occurs when terms are used for concepts that have no clear dividing lines or where no bright-line rule can be established for moral judgments. Take the following example:

Devious Philosopher: Would you agree that a newborn baby has a right to life and should not be killed?

Pro-Choice advocate: Yes, of course.

Philosopher: Would you also agree that the difference of one minute in terms of that baby's development cannot make the difference between having a right to life and its not having a right to life?

Advocate: What do you mean?

Philosopher: Well, if the baby has a right to life in virtue of its mental state—this is what distinguishes a newborn baby from a zygote, for example—will the difference of one minute in the nine month process of gestation make a difference between that baby having a right to life and his not having such a right? Will there be much change in that baby's state of mental development in the course of one minute?

Advocate: Well, no, of course not. One minute can never make such an important difference in development that, at one minute a baby has a right to life but, at the previous minute, it did not. No, one minute does not make a difference.

Philosopher: Very well. You have agreed that a newborn baby has a right to life and that one minute cannot make the difference between having a right to life and not having a right to life. It follows from these two premises that the baby one moment before birth also has a right to life. Correct?

Advocate: (Edgy) Well I suppose so.

Philosopher: And since a baby one minute before birth has a right to life and because one minute never makes a difference, the baby two minutes before birth has a right to life also. Right?

Advocate: Well, I don't

Philosopher: Doesn't it follow from your previous logic?

Advocate: Well, I suppose.

Philosopher: And you see where the logic leads. We can follow this chain of reasoning back to the two-celled blastocyst stage with the conclusion that it, too, has a right to life.

Advocate: There's something wrong here, I know it!

And, indeed, there is something wrong. What is wrong is that many small changes add up to big changes. The logic of the argument as framed cannot account for this real-world fact. (The same argument might have been made from the opposite standpoint: if one accepts that a newly fertilized ovum does *not* have a right to life and that one minute will never make a moral difference, then the same ovum lacks this right at one minute past conception. And on down the chain of reasoning until we are concluding that a newborn baby—or, for that matter, an eighteen-year-old child—has no right to life.

The Sorites paradox is sometimes called the "argument of the beard" in recognition of this problem: While one hair never makes the difference between having a beard and not having a beard, such that pulling one hair out of a one thousand hair beard will still leave a beard, if we keep pulling hairs there comes a point somewhere along the way—who can say where exactly?—where there is no longer a beard. Whether this point is reached at two hundred hairs, twenty hairs, or two hairs is a matter of semantic debate. But *somewhere* along the way the beard no longer exists.

In the debate between vegetarians and nonvegetarians, the nonvegetarian will sometimes commit the Sorites fallacy in a variety of ways. One way in which the fallacy is committed is by arguing, as the author above did, that because we cannot draw a neat line between the conscious and the nonconscious, the plant must be conscious and, thus, there is no moral advantage to being a vegetarian. The writer might as well have drawn the conclusion that because there is no clear dividing line between the conscious and the nonconscious, rocks are conscious as well.

Alternatively, rather than making an empirical claim about the mental state of plants, the objection may simply argue, as a moral matter, that killing is killing. It does not matter where along the evolutionary line it happens, the objection holds, it is no better to kill plants than to kill animals.

This is, of course, the grossest of logical fallacies. Language does not mirror the world. It cannot begin to. The infinite gradations within and between things in the world cannot be captured adequately by the finite and discrete concepts we employ to describe the world. Nor can language reflect accurately our intuitive moral sense, which tells us that, as the object of our moral propositions changes, so too will our moral judgments. We do not treat rocks, plants, insects, animals and humans all similarly. Just as there are gradations in the state of each type of thing in the world, there are refinements in our moral position regarding these things. It is this same phenomenon which that leads most people to accept that a newborn baby has a right to life while a fertilized ovum does not. All along the way between the ovum and the baby, changes are occurring. Somewhere along the way, lines must be drawn. It is the problem of line drawing that is presumably what much, if not all, of the fighting is about in the abortion controversy.

The proponent of the line-drawing objection is not even being consistent when he makes the argument that killing is killing, whether the victim be plant or animal. He is not consistent because he himself draws these lines every day. He believes it is permissible to kill animals but not humans. Why should the vegetarian not be permitted the same convenience, drawing the line (for better reasons) between plants and animals, rather than between animals and humans?

In the end, the vegetarian needs a criterion to distinguish the edible from the inedible, a reason for drawing the line where she draws it. A woman I once knew who was a vegetarian used to say that she wouldn't eat anything with a face. While this has an undeniable appeal, more precise criteria were considered in chapter 2. For the utilitarian, it is the ability to *suffer*—to experience pain—that distinguishes protected species from those that may be eaten. The Australian utilitarian philosopher Peter Singer draws the line of "equal consideration" between crustaceans—lobsters, crabs, and shrimp—which can feel pain, and mollusks—clams, oysters, and mussels—which he argues do not feel pain. Others have pointed out that the octopus, which is a mollusk, displays changes in emotion by changes in skin color. They are also clever enough to unscrew a jar lid to get to food.[15]

Deontologists such as animal rights philosopher Tom Regan, on the other hand, use the "subject of a life" criterion. Any creature that *experiences life*, that is sentient in the widest sense—any being that is "the subject of a life"—should be protected. This criterion would include most species in the animal kingdom, perhaps including insects, while excluding plants and some microscopic multicelled animals, bacteria, and others. (See chapter 2.) This criterion results in a wider net being cast: lower forms of animal life not covered by the utilitarian criterion are protected by the "subject of a life" criterion.[16]

Once we are clear on why, as vegetarians, we do not eat animals, we can develop our criterion for distinguishing protected species from those that may be consumed. Once this is done, the line-drawing objections lose all import.

"Are Those Leather Shoes?": The "All or Nothing" Approach and the Fallacy of Black and White Thinking

Another common bane of the vegetarian's existence concerns the attempt by some of our carnivorous friends to seize upon any practice or habit that can be even vaguely construed as a sign of inconsistency—or, better yet, hypocrisy—on the part of the vegetarian. With barely veiled glee, the nonvegetarian will spot and point out the vegetarian's leather belt, triumphantly announcing, with a smirk, a shake of the finger, and a mock sense of revelation, that leather comes from cows, after all. Another example finds the vegetarian at a weaker moment, a victim of heat, humidity—an available rolled-up newspaper. With these forces in place, the vegetarian may successfully swat the fly that had patiently circled his nose for the previous twenty minutes. At such moments the nonvegetarian is readily on hand reminding us that, yes, strictly speaking, flies are animals, too.

Do you use products that are tested on animals before they are marketed? Do you still eat eggs, drink milk, or consume cheese or other dairy products? These also come from animals who are caged, debeaked, force-molted, exploited, and ultimately slaughtered. The unrelenting carnivore is fast to point out these gaps. As such, this type of objection is less an argument for the value of an omnivorous diet than it is an unabashed quest for rhetorical revenge, a last-ditch effort on the part of the meat eater not to maintain the pretense of logical superiority, but merely to deny the vegetarian this same advantage.

How are all these various habits and practices to be reconciled with the vegetarian philosophy, to the extent such a philosophy exists? Those vegetarians who are motivated primarily by health concerns do not have this problem, of course. They can freely respond that they care not a whit for animals or animal rights, and that their reason for being vegetarian is purely "selfish." But as most vegetarians are motivated at least in part by concerns for the welfare of animals, most do not have this rhetorical luxury. Some other response is necessary, lest the vegetarian face the most serious charges of his philosophical or moral inquisitors: inconsistency or hypocrisy.

The answer that must be offered may not completely satisfy the strict philosophical rationalists in the audience. Yet it is an imminently practical, real-world response. Let me illustrate with a story from another moral context: Some years ago, during the Ethiopian famine of 1983, I became involved in a discussion with an acquaintance on the propriety of sending relief. I remarked that I had felt bad that I had not sent money to the relief effort that was underway, that perhaps I should send something after all. My acquaintance responded that he would not consider such a course of action. When I inquired why, he stated that, if he were going to help at all, he would have to dedicate himself fully to the cause. He would have to sell the business, pack up the family, and move to Ethiopia to assist in the relief effort. As this was impossible at the moment for other reasons, he declined to do anything, even by way of sending money.

Mildly surprised by this response—a simple plea that he was broke, or lazy, or just didn't care would have ended the matter—I asked why he had ruled out doing some small part, even if it were impractical to devote his life to the cause. He merely shook his head: if you can't do it all, why do anything? In fact, those who do some small bit are the real hypocrites, he maintained. They attempt to assuage their middle-class guilt by sending ten dollars to an effort that they then immediately forget about, satisfied that they have done their bit. This, he continued, is the selfish and cowardly way out. Better to simply accept the guilt that comes with doing nothing.

My friend was engaging in the fallacy of black and white thinking. The fallacy is not a fallacy of logical form; it occurs not as the result of faulty logical structure of an argument but as the result of a false premise. The false premise is the premise that holds that there are only two options available, usually two polar extremes (e.g., "you are either with us or against us," or as Camus wrote, "there are in this world only two things: victims and pestilences and one must do all one can so as not to join forces with the latter"). My friend's response was to deny that any middle ground was practical. The meat eater does the same when he torments his herbivorous chum with this objection.

There are basically two responses the vegetarian can make to the all-or-nothing objection. The objection usually is motivated by the charge of inconsistency of the variety, "You say you don't eat meat because you say you can't condone the abuse of animals, so why do you eat eggs/use leather/swat flies, etc." One response, depending upon the reason for being a vegetarian, is to point out that there is no inconsistency at all. For example, flies may fall outside the criterion used for distinguishing the protected class of animals: if the criterion used provides that one will not kill animals who possess certain higher mental states such as desires, wants, and expectations for example, then assuming flies have no such mental states, there would be nothing inconsistent with a vegetarian's swatting insects.

Of course, the criterion itself may be challenged—for example, why is the ability to have desires, wants, and expectations important to whether a certain species should be protected? Or, the nonvegetarian may accept the criterion but claim that the species in question does in fact have the requisite attributes such that it should be protected—for example, "How do you know flies have no desires, wants, and expectations?" But if the vegetarian can meet these replies, his argument will find itself in safe logical waters.

This same approach may be played out in a variety of similar contexts. The vegetarian may object to killing animals but may find nothing wrong with animals "paying their way," as long as they are treated properly. Thus, the vegetarian may buy eggs or milk from dairy farmers who let their hens or cows live more or less naturally. Similarly, there would be nothing wrong with wearing leather, from the vegetarian's standpoint, if the leather came from an animal that had died naturally. (Recently, leather goods manufacturers have responded to the animal rights cause by marketing leather from animals that have died naturally though, the question remains, how the vegetarian could know this with certainty.) In short, the vegetarian is not necessarily inconsistent by engaging in some of these various acts.

The second response open to the vegetarian is to admit the charge of inconsistency. The vegetarian may be strictly opposed to all forms of killing, even the most primitive of insects, and still may not adopt the practice of the orthodox Jains, which consists of walking about with a broom, sweeping the bugs from one's path. She may be opposed to killing and yet might accept the gift of a leather belt. The point is that, while this behavior may not be completely consistent, and while the conscientious vegetarian should make every reasonable effort to conform all her habits to her stated beliefs, complete consistency is not always possible in the real world. What is important is that she is making a real effort to live by her beliefs. In short, she may not always be completely consistent, but is the only other alternative to absolute consistency to make no attempt at all? Is it not better to make even modest strides in the direction to which one aspires, even if one cannot always reach one's aspiration, than to make no attempt at all?

To answer this question in the negative is to condemn oneself to a life of barren, amoral consistency, an existence principled, in some empty rational sense, but entirely without commitment. In essence, it is better by far to have your principles and go some way, if not the whole way, toward meeting them than having no principles at all. This may be the best response to the all-or-nothing objection.

Lost Jobs and Revenue: The Economic Objection

Probably the most serious objection to be considered here is the argument that, if vegetarianism were to become widely accepted, the impact upon the economy of our nation and other nations around the world would be devastating. Jobs would be lost in meat producing, packaging, and distributing industries, along with the jobs of those working in related industries, such as those who produce feed grain and those employed at fast food restaurants. This, in turn, would presumably have a great impact upon the the economy in terms of tax revenue, secondary economic influences, bankruptcies, and so on. Too much is riding on meat, the meat industry would have us believe, to embrace vegetarianism as the new *modus vivendi*.

There are three responses to the economic objection. First, economic considerations may be outweighed by more important moral considerations. Second, the objection has been grossly overplayed: the loss of jobs and revenue that would occur with the widespread acceptance of vegetarianism would be gradual, relatively insignificant in number, and offset by an increase in jobs related to food production and sales geared to vegetarian alternatives. Finally, there would be great economic advantages, both in terms of health care costs and in terms of ecological harm that would be prevented, that would dwarf any negative economic consequences of reduction or curtailment of the meat industry.

The first response to the economic objection holds quite simply that, even if there were certain untoward economic consequences to result from a reduction in meat eating, more important moral considerations may require equal or greater weight. The tobacco industry has undoubtedly witnessed a decline in jobs since the government policy to warn consumers of the health risks inherent in cigarette smoking took effect. The decline in jobs and other revenue related to tobacco and cigarette production were consequences we were willing to accept given the harmful effects of these products. Similarly, the drug trade provides an income for hundreds of thousands of farmers around the world, particularly South American growers of coca leaves. In addition, the legalization of drugs would result in the creation of thousands of jobs related to the production, marketing, and distribution of drugs in this country. Tax revenues and gross national product arguably would be similarly benefited by drug legalization, at least in the short term.

So why does the government spend billions of dollars each year fighting, rather than legitimizing, the drug trade? The obvious answer: because there are more fundamental issues at stake than economic issues. Where lives are at stake, economic issues become secondary. Why should the conclusion be any different with the case for vegetarianism? Whether the lives we refer to are those of the millions of people who suffer or die each year as the result of diseases, such as cancer or heart disease, which are linked to the consumption of meat, or the lives of the animals who die to perpetuate these human maladies, the policy remains the same.

Moreover, the economic objection has been greatly overstated. The meat industry is not the employer of millions it once was. Seventy years ago, the meat-processing industry was the nation's second-largest employer.[17] Today there are roughly only 135,000 men and women employed in the industry. Hundreds of thousands of jobs have already been lost over the past few decades as the meat-processing industry has become highly automated, labor intensive, and dominated by three major corporations that together slaughter over 70 percent of the feedlot cattle in the United States.[18] It is ironic, to say the least, that the call to corporate profits which has resulted in a killing process so streamlined that it puts the automotive industry to shame, should justify the gradual loss of many more jobs than exist today in the industry, while a concern for human health, the environment, and the lives of millions of animals slaughtered each year should be overlooked in the name of the worker.

Nor are these jobs typically stable or long-term. Because of the unsafe and unsanitary working conditions endemic of the slaughterhouses, job turnover is high, as much as 43 percent per month in some plants, a fact that also helps insulate the industry from unionization.[19] Injuries on the job are at least three times the national average. With the highly automated assembly-line process designed to give employees as little control over the process as possible, workers make thousands of "cuts" a day on lines that process three hundred cattle per hour. Some cutters must make five cuts every fifteen seconds, a pace that results in a huge number of muscular and orthopedic injuries.[20]

In his book, *Beyond Beef*, author-activist Jeremy Rifkin documents both the dark political history of the meat industry and its current economic status. After decsribing the horrible conditions of the slaughterhouse of the past, Rifkin writes:

> Little has changed in the meat-packing industry since Upton Sinclair's telling account of working conditions in the slaughterhouses at the turn of the century. Working conditions are still hazardous and unsanitary. Workers are still mercilessly exploited by management. The companies continue to foster inhumane practices on the kill floors and in the chill rooms. The conditions are often primitive, even ghoulish. Says Elanor Kennedy of the UFCW, "A meat-packing plant is like nothing you've ever seen or could imagine. It's like a vision of hell."[21]

Even if the nation converts largely or wholly to a meatless diet, the process will be gradual. Thus, any jobs that are lost in the meat-packing industry will occur slowly, often by attrition, after the retirement or the voluntary movement of workers. As for workers in the jobs related to or dependent upon meat consumption, for example, those working in fast-food restaurants, as the populace shifts to a vegetarian diet, so too will business adapt, offering meatless alternatives to hamburgers, hot dogs and other meat-oriented meals. Thus, the only thing to be affected by a wholesale conversion to vegetarianism on the part of the public will be what goes under the bun, not who serves the sandwich.

Finally, to the extent anything remains of the economic objection—to the extent a conversion to a meatless diet can be said
to have any negative economic effects in terms of lost jobs and
revenue—these effects must be weighed in good utilitarian fashion against the positive economic results of such a transition.
First, the impact upon health care costs would be considerable.
With the elimination of perhaps the greatest cause of heart disease and certain forms of cancer, along with other deleterious
effects of meat eating upon health, the amount of money saved
in terms of health care costs, lowered insurance costs, fewer
workdays lost to these diseases, and such, would reach tens of
billions of dollars. (See chapter 3)

Moreover, with the curtailment of cattle grazing, vast areas
of land in the western United States would be opened up and
could be put to more productive use. Similarly, the huge government largesse in the form of tax breaks and subsidies paid to
cattle ranchers, along with the loss of money to the government
as the result of token leasing fees paid by ranchers for the right
to graze their cattle on government land, all well documented in
Rifkin's book, must be factored into the economic equation.[22]
Finally, the amount of money that could be saved by preventing
the land erosion, deforestation, and water pollution that are very
largely the result of current mass-grazing practices would be almost inestimable, but easily hundreds of billions of dollars. (See
chapter 4)

Consequently, even if we were to ignore the noneconomic
benefits to the health of our nation, to the environment and to
our world generally as the result of a widescale transition to
vegetarianism, far from militating against adoption of a meatless
diet, economic considerations overwhelmingly favor it. In short,
the economic argument speaks powerfully in favor of the case
for vegetarianism.

Other Objections

Very few good ideas have ever been accepted, upon their introduction, without first encountering a certain amount of ridicule,
derision, or outright disregard on the part of society at large. It

is unreasonable to expect that the case for vegetarianism should be any different.

People are, perhaps by nature, conservative in their response to calls for change, whether this be social, political, or of a more personal nature. This conservatism manifests itself in human ignorance—literally, "ignor-ance." People resist change either by ignoring the need for change or by ignoring the information that would permit, even propel, change. Ignorance is the preferred method of resisting change because it is the only device that permits, without sacrifice to good conscience, moral inertia—that is, the propensity to refuse to confront the need for change.

This is nowhere more true than in the case for vegetarianism. In this chapter we have examined a number of arguments raised by nonvegetarians. Some of these objections have appeared plausible at first though, upon closer examination, they have proven weak, false, or misleading. Other objections considered have been of a more rhetorical nature. The last two objections to be considered here are arguments, like some we have already seen, that are motivated by moral inertia. Both objections will acknowledge, albeit grudgingly, that vegetarianism is a good thing, but seek to raise some other defense to their proponent's transition to vegetarianism. Both are motivated by moral inertia to the extent that they are simply rhetorical ways, on the part of their advocates, of resisting taking action.

The first of these two objections argues that, while vegetarianism might not be a bad idea, there are simply more important things to worry about in this very imperfect world. With the plight of the poor and the homeless, the ill and the elderly, with the seemingly intractable problems of the inner city, drugs, crime, war, and famine, to mention but a few, how can we think about becoming vegetarians? Surely there are more important things to put our energies toward in this world. As one author makes the objection:

> It is a well-known phenomenon that people's hearts go out quickly and spontaneously to pet animals and to infants of all species, perceived as utterly defenseless and innocently lovable. Sadly, they do not warm as readily to young children or to adolescents in need. . . . Still less do they respond to the plight of the suffering millions of adult human beings around the globe.[23]

It is not that the proponent of this objection typically *does* anything about these other problems. Rather, the objection is a foil, a subterfuge—though a particularly effective subterfuge because it purports to come from the standpoint of activism.

But this argument falls completely short as an objection to vegetarianism for two reasons. First, vegetarianism is in no way *inconsistent* with an active stance on these other problems. Becoming a vegetarian does not in any way detract from one's ability to address these other problems. Second, as we have witnessed in the previous chapters, becoming a vegetarian is one way of fighting at least some of these problems. Whether the problems with which one is preoccupied are world famine, poverty, or the environment, vegetarianism is one way of personally doing something, of making a difference.

This leads to a consideration of the second objection from moral inertia. The objection asks rhetorically: What can I do? How will becoming a vegetarian—one person's stand—change anything? Note that this is an objection from despair in the truest sense. There is no objection to vegetarianism nor is there anything more important one wishes to do. Rather, the person making this objection, either by apathy or by sheer helplessness, wholly renounces his individual effort and effect as a moral agent in the world.

By becoming a vegetarian, one immediately becomes an example to others. This can have a tremendous influence upon other people who may be similarly inclined. A recent survey indicates that most vegetarians can point to at least one other person whom they have influenced in making the transition to vegetarianism.[24] Since these people may influence still others, the attenuated effects of one person's decision in terms of the decisions of others may be very significant.

Moreover, each person's decision not to eat meat directly affects the lives of numerous animals. As one author has written, "every person who becomes a vegetarian is directly responsible for saving between forty and ninety-five creatures every year, depending on her or his level of meat consumption. It is the single most effective step one could take to assist individual animals."[25]

While the effect might not be quite as direct as this writer suggests—some of the animals one would have eaten might have been slaughtered nevertheless, even if only to go to waste in the supermarket freezer—the indirect effect is still great. As more people become vegetarians, the market is forced to adapt by offering more vegetarian alternatives, with a consequent reduction in the number of animals slaughtered each year. As we noted earlier in the book, for every 1 percent of the population who become vegetarian, as many animals are saved each year as all those used in all forms of commercial, medical, and scientific experimentation.

Finally, of course, the person who makes the transition to vegetarianism has the greatest effect upon herself or himself. In terms of increased energy and vitality, improved health and all of the other salutary mental and physical effects, the case for vegetarianism is compelling.

There are undoubtedly other objections that the vegetarian will confront but the arguments mentioned here are the most common. Other objections are variations on some of the themes we have seen in this chapter. I believe we have covered a great deal of the field here, however. None, it appears, can mitigate the case for vegetarianism as it has been developed throughout this book.

If the case for vegetarianism is as clear or as compelling as we have argued, how is it that so many, in so many different cultures down through history and all over the world, could have arrived at the opposite conclusion? Are they simply wrong? Or, is there a kind of "moral progress" that we as a people, as a nation—perhaps as a species—have undergone? Are vegetarians at the forefront of a kind of "moral evolution?" These are questions to be considered in the next and last chapter.

Chapter Seven

Vegetarianism and
Moral Progress

In the previous six chapters, we have argued that the case for vegetarianism, for the objective moral superiority of the vegetarian diet over a diet that includes meat, is clear from virtually every moral perspective and from the standpoint of every relevant consideration. Whether one is a utilitarian, a rights and duty-oriented deontologist, or even a self-seeking egoist, vegetarianism poses the best answer to the question of the proper diet. Similarly, whether one is primarily concerned with her own health or the health of others, with issues relating to world hunger or to the environment, or whether the primary concern is with the lives and well-being of the creatures who wind up as our food, the answer is the same. Indeed, rarely in the annals of moral history has there been a moral question with so few conflicting or countervailing arguments, with such a univocal solution, and with so many roads of ethical consideration all pointing in the same direction. The case for vegetarianism is clear beyond a reasonable moral doubt.

But if this is true, why have so few people down through history and today relinquished meat? Why do the great majority of individuals in our own culture and in other cultures around the world continue to eat meat? Why have most cultures endorsed and even enshrined meat eating as a sign of, and prerequisite to, the good life? And, perhaps most importantly from a moral standpoint, should the assent to meat eating of this great majority of people and cultures constitute a kind of presumption in favor of the moral permissibility of eating meat? After all, who are the few to call into question the practices of a great majority, particularly where these same practices have scarcely been questioned previously? In short, how can a practice be so obviously wrong when so few have even thought twice about it?

A preliminary answer may be that it is precisely because so few have called it into question or thought twice about it, that the practice of meat eating has survived. Before elaborating on this conclusion, however, more needs to be said by way of answering the question: How can the vegetarian be so certain she is right when so few appear to agree with her?

Cultural Relativism, or "The Majority Is Always Right"

The vegetarian must admit that he is in a distinct minority today. In the United States perhaps nine million people consider themselves vegetarian, less than 4 percent of the total population.[1] And this number probably represents a high-water mark in the number of adherents to a vegetarian diet in a modern Western nation. With the exception of a few cultures at various points in history that have adopted vegetarian diets, some for religious reasons and some by virtue of sheer economic or natural necessity, meat eating has been with us since our primordial, evolutionary past. As we saw in chapter 3, even our prehominoidal ancestors hunted and killed small game.

It is interesting to note that the development of civilization itself required us to relinquish, at least partially, the life of hunting for the life of agriculture. The symbolic connection between agriculture and a diet consisting of cultivated vegetable products, on one hand, and the development of civilization, on the other, has sometimes been represented as a kind of feminization of humankind. Both agriculture and cultural achievement generally require the development of such Apollonian (and "female") virtues as patience, nurturance, long-term planning, and the creation and maintenance of advanced systems of social organization. Contrast with this is the Dionysian predilection to aggression, sport, warfare, and all the supposed male virtues. Hunting is masculine and so is its reward, a diet of meat. Indeed, this association of meat with the masculine may explain not only why

70 percent of all vegetarians are women,[2] but also why meat eating has endured and flourished in our own society and in other cultures historically. Meat is the food of competition, rather than cooperation, war rather than peace, dominance rather than harmonious coexistence. The psychology of meat eating has permeated the fabric of our political history and our culture and shaped what one author has called "the sexual politics of meat eating."[3]

But should the fact that the majority have never viewed meat eating as morally impermissible be relevant to our own moral determination of the propriety of vegetarianism? To answer this, we must distinguish two ways in which the majority's acceptance of a diet consisting of meat might be relevant. The first of the two views says something like, "Any practice, including meat eating is permissible because the majority says it is permissible." In other words, meat eating is permitted because the majority says it violates no moral standard, and because the culture as a whole permits and endorses it.

This view, which holds that what is right is what a culture (or the majority in a culture) says is right, is a form of cultural relativism. What is "right" from culture to culture may vary with the practices of each respective culture, according to this view, but within each culture accepted practices set the norm. Thus, in contemporary American culture, as in most other cultures around he world, most people see nothing wrong with meat eating; consequently, there *is* nothing wrong with meat eating.

As we saw in chapter 1, this form of moral reasoning is highly problematic. Aside from the fact that it entails that there are no truly morally objective claims claims about the rightness and wrongness of actions *independent* of what we may think about them the view that the majority is always right requires us to say, for example, that in traditional Hindu culture, wife burning was morally permissible. Similarly, there was nothing wrong with slavery in the antebellum South, or the extermination of the Jews in Nazi Germany, or racial or sexual discrimination anywhere it occurred with such frequency that it could be called a "social practice." In short, if something is permissible *simply because* the majority believes it to be, we can never appeal to some other standard outside the cultural norm to demonstrate that the practice is wrong. By this definition, the social reformer will always be "wrong" because, by definition, she is seeking to change some prevailing existing practice. Cultural relativism stops moral reasoning before it begins; it is the antithesis of moral reasoning.

Perhaps, however, a second, more moderate view is possible. What if a majority's assent to a particular practice is merely *evidence* that there is nothing wrong with the practice. In other words, it is not that the majority is always right by definition, such that prevailing cultural practices are deemed to be correct simply because they are prevailing cultural practices, but rather that the beliefs of the majority should command some sort of respect. After all, cultural practices develop over centuries. There is bound to be some moral wisdom inherent in practices that have endured and evolved over the course of long periods of time. Moreover, where a majority of individuals believe a certain practice to be perfectly morally legitimate, who are the few to presume to overrule the judgment of the majority and, indeed, a supermajority in this case with their own?

While there is perhaps a good case to be made for the view that there should be something like a presumption in favor of existing cultural practices, the presumption should nevertheless be a rebuttable one. As we have just mentioned, we now typically think the majority was often wrong in the past, whether Hindu wife burning or Greek infanticide is the subject of modern hindsight. Particularly in the area of moral speculation, majorities have proven regularly resistant to what might have been viewed as intermeddling attempts at reform by a few. Many beliefs that are today held with the conviction of immutable truth were at one time or another ridiculed and dismissed. The case for vegetarianism may join this group of firmly held convictions at some point in the future. As Albert Schweitzer wrote in an essay entitled, "The Sacredness of All Lives" early this century:

> It is the fate of every truth to be the object of ridicule when it is first acclaimed. Today it is considered an exaggeration to proclaim constant respect for every form of life as being the serious demand of a national ethic. But the time is coming when people will be amazed that the human race was so long before it recognized that thoughtless injury to life is incompatible with real ethics. Ethics is, in its unqualified form, extended responsibility with regard to everything that has life.[4]

The majority is neither always wrong, as Voltaire reputedly maintained, nor are they always right, as the cultural relativist claims. While long-standing cultural practices deserve a presumption in their favor such that they should not be overturned with minimal consideration, there is also something to be said for the notion that certain practices may be *too* ingrained such that they are not even carefully examined by those who adhere to them. Where strong evidence exists for changing a social practice, as surely it does with the case for vegetarianism, the reformer has met the burden of her presumption. Social habit should yield to moral imperative.

Moral Objectivity and the Idea of Moral Progress

The question as to whether collectively we have made any moral progress from the dawn of civilization down to the present time is an issue that finds itself hotly contested by philosophers, historians, and others. Of course, if one is a moral subjectivist, moral progress is an illusion, impossible as a matter of principle. If there exist no objective standards in the world, neither can there be some objective goal toward which we advance. There may be movement always, but the idea of progress implies that something is getting better. Again, however, if there are no goods and bads, rights and wrongs, there can be nothing that is better and nothing that is worse, at least from a moral point of view. Philosophically, the claim to moral progress presupposes the truth of moral realism.

Putting the philosophical issue to the side for the moment, even if one adheres to a belief in some form of moral realism, there remains a serious question whether, as a matter of historical fact, we have made any genuine moral progress over the course of the last few thousand years. At least one historian has argued that moral progress has come nowhere near to keeping pace with our material progress, and that we are, on the whole, not much better morally than our earliest civilized ancestors.[5] Whatever view one takes of this question as an historic matter, clearly most people would agree that certain developments represent genuine progress, in some significant moral sense. The

abolition of slavery and recognition of the rights of women surely
must count for progress in the relevant way, even if these advances may be offset by other, less-hopeful developments.

Most generally, however, how do we recognize moral progress
historically and in our culture today? How do we know an example of moral progress when we see it?

Throughout this book I have argued that there are objective
moral truths that can be assessed by recourse, first, to the dictates of deontological thought and then, second, by a weighing
of the costs and benefits to any proposed scheme in utilitarian
fashion. To the extent that we act in accord with these principles, we advance the cause of cultural progress. Thus, one way
of knowing whether there is moral progress is by appeal to traditional moral philosophy in determining whether our actions
meet the criteria that emerge from rational analysis.

Nevertheless, there may be disagreements about particular issues, especially when there are conflicting moral claims and countervailing consequences of taking a specific action. To take only
the most controversial of such issues as a contemporary matter,
does the legalization and increased availability of abortion in the
United States constitute a form of moral progress or an absolute
moral regression, as some claim? The arguments on both sides,
whether from the standpoint of the rights of women or those of
the unborn, need not be reiterated here. The point is that we are
often uncertain, and equally often disagree, about whether a particular move is in the direction of genuine moral progress.

With respect to the case for vegetarianism, however, are there
many who will argue that eliminating meat from the diet is a
definite step in the *wrong* direction? While many will undoubtedly maintain that vegetarianism is not *morally obligatory*, most
defenders of meat eating will still acknowledge that a world in
which everyone voluntarily gave up the eating of meat is no
worse a place to live. Moreover, it might be suspected that most
of these would even grudgingly admit that a world without killing for meat would be a downright better place to live. Indeed,
while the prevailing view of the meat-and-potato conservative is
that killing animals for meat is not really so bad, I have seen no
argument from anyone, once fears regarding the healthfulness of
the vegetarian diet are allayed, that the practice of killing and

eating animals is affirmatively better than not doing so at all. The reason for this is obvious: such an argument would be patently absurd, contrary to all our other views about the sacredness of life, human or otherwise.

The point in all this is that, even where our life-long habits and prejudices may prevent us from going so far as to say meat eating is wrong, nevertheless, we recognize that a world in which universal vegetarianism held sway would be better or, at least, no worse, than the world we have now. And this is a significant concession in a culture where the propriety of killing animals for food has scarcely been challenged.

There is, however, an even deeper sense in which we seek, individually and collectively, to contribute to the imperative of moral progress. There is a more profound significance to the pursuit of moral progress than adherence to rational principles. Most basically, genuine moral progress both requires and promotes our own self-improvement. It requires us to be, and in turn makes us, better human beings. Thus, moral progress is not merely evinced by external changes in our behavior, it is internal, psychological even spiritual in nature.

Moral progress in a *contingent* sense takes place every time we change the external conditions of our existence, making the world a bit better for others and perhaps ourselves in the process. But *real* moral progress entails changing the human soul itself. It requires that *we*, rather than the conditions of our existence, have gotten better. This is the difference, for example, between being more generous because one has more to give, or because one's survival is not jeopardized by giving to others, on one hand, and being more generous because one simply wants to better the lives of others, whether or not one's life circumstances makes this easily accomplished. Most fundamentally, there simply has been no essential moral progress if the goodness of our inclinations wanes with our fortunes. Put simply, true moral progress is progress of the soul.

If the claims of moral progress can be boiled down to one factor psychologically if there is one process with which moral progress is synonymous it is this: the willingness and ability to view every situation from the perspective of the Other. It is a sensitivity to the claims of others other races, other sexes, and, now, other species. Wherever a creature may lay claim to being a sentient participant in life and in the world, it has a claim to moral consideration. The essence of moral progress is the recognition of this fact and the commitment to live by the standards it imposes.

A transition to vegetarianism would be a mark of moral progress insofar as it represents an overcoming of social convention in the name of the interests of other animals. As Gandhi wrote, "I do feel that spiritual progress does demand at some stage that we should cease to kill our fellow creatures for the satisfaction of our bodily wants."[6] Vegetarianism may be both a prerequisite to, and a mark of moral progress. As Thoreau stated in *Walden*: "I have no doubt that it is part of the destiny of the human race, in its gradual improvement, to leave off eating animals, as surely as the savage tribes have left off eating each other when they came in contact with the more civilized."[7]

Is Meat Eating Wrong?:
The Moral Dilemma of the Vegetarian

The vegetarian finds himself in something of a moral dilemma in contemporary society: Either there is something seriously wrong with meat eating or there is not. If there is not anything greatly wrong with killing animals for food, then what is all the fuss about? Live and let live is perhaps a bad choice of words, considering the implications of the position at least among humans.

More than a few vegetarians adopt this position. For those who do, the decision not to eat meat is simply a matter of individual preference; no moral blame, sanction, or disapprobation goes with meat eating. But if, on the other hand, there is something in some sense morally wrong with eating meat or, to put it in a positive manner, if vegetarianism is morally preferable, then what should the vegetarian do about it? Here is where the real dilemma begins.

Does acceptance of the view that meat eating is morally problematic require the vegetarian to take the position of the moral "hard-liner?" Should the vegetarian do all within her power to renounce even fight the culture of meat eating? For example, should she refuse to eat at restaurants that serve meat, to attend social gatherings where meat will be eaten, to date people who are nonvegetarian, and so on? How far should the vegetarian go in proclaiming and maintaining her avowed principles?

The alternative course to that of the moral hard-liner is that of compromise, example and gentle persuasion. This approach prescribes living by one's own principles but living within the world as it exists. The advocate of gentle persuasion calls for vegetarians to change hearts by their example. It recommends against foisting one's principles off on unwilling others, but rather, counsels bringing about change in a thousand quiet ways.

Proponents of both positions share with advocates of other varied moral values a fundamental disagreement regarding the moral legitimacy of the two approaches. The hard-liner has what he believes to be a fundamental moral objection to the methods of the gentle persuader namely, that the latter is selling out, or has failed to take seriously the significance of the wrongness of meat eating. Meat eating entails the slaughter of billions of animals a year, after all. How can the gentle persuader take a position that falls anything short of strongly condemning the practice of meat eating?

The gentle persuader, in turn, has a practical objection to the methods of the hard-liner. If the object is to change the hearts and minds, not to mention the behavior of others, alienating them is surely not the most effective way of achieving this goal. It is by example, and by participation, not by coercion and indignation, that others will respond.

It is the method of the gentle persuader that is to be recommended here. The question is an issue of means and not ends: What is the best way to bring about social change?

Presumably, the vegetarian can affect a change by taking part in all that life has to offer and by positively influencing those with whom she comes in contact. Steadfastly maintaining one's principles does little good if those who violate them are out of earshot. Moreover, those who eat meat are not moral villains. More likely than not, they have simply never thought about, nor have they been exposed to, the intricacies and complexities of this issue. The vegetarian seeking to change people's values is best served by enlightening, not chastising, by representing an example, rather than by alienating or sanctimoniously condemning the habits of those who still eat meat.

I share the conviction of many before, including Thoreau, Shaw, Einstein, and Gandhi, that the human race will one day, perhaps not too far in the distant future, look back upon our earlier practice of eating animals as yet another obstacle that had to be overcome on the road to our humanity. This book has been my small but heartfelt contribution to this cause.

Notes

Introduction

1. Tom Regan, *The Thee Generation* (Philadelphia: Temple University Press, 1991), 35; Laurence Pringle, *The Animal Rights Controversy* (San Diego: Harcourt, Brace, 1989), 44–45.
2. Pringle, *The Animal Rights Controversy*, 28.
3. Steven Rosen, *Food for the Spirit*: *Vegetarianism and the World Religious* (San Diego: Bala/Entourage Books, 1990), iii–iv.
4. Pringle, *The Animal Rights Controversy*, 39.
5. Paul Amato and Sonia A. Partridge, *The New Vegetarians*: *Promoting Health and Protecting Life* (New York: Plenum Press, 1989), 1.
6. Ibid., 34.
7. Ibid., 34–35.
8. Ibid., 2–4.

Chapter 2

1. Steven Rosen, *Food for the Spirit*: *Vegetarianism and the World Religious* (San Diego: Bala/Entourage books, 1990), 19.
2. Ibid., 15.
3. For an interesting overview of the history of the relationship between humans and animals, see Monica Hutchings and Mavis Caver, *Man's Dominion*: *Our Violation of the Animal World* (London: Rupert Hart-Davis, 1970); for a compilations of essays on a similar topic, see Richard Knowles Morris and Michael W. Fox, *On the Fifth Day*: *Animal Rights and Human Ethics* (Washington: Acropolis Books Ltd., 1978).
4. A recent survey indicates that the great majority found the transition to vegetarianism easy. Amato and Partridge, *The New Vegetarians*, 32–34.
5. Bart Gruzalski, "The Case against Raising and Killing Animals

for Food," in Harlan B. Miller and William H. Williams, *Ethics and Animals* (Clifton, N.J.: Humana, 1983).

6. Ibid.

7. Jeremy Rifkin, *Beyond Beef* (New York: Dutton, 1992).

8. Jan Narveson, "Animal Rights Revisited," in Miller and Williams, *Ethics and Animals*, 52.

9. Michael Allen Fox, *The Case for Animal Experimentation* (Berkeley: University of California Press, 1986), 63–67.

10. Ibid., 63–67.

11. Narveson, "Animal Rights Revisited," 58–59.

12. Pringle, *The Animal Rights Controversy*, 21.

13. Regan, *The Thee Generation* 46–48.

14. Narveson, "Animal Rights Revisited," 58.

15. Regan, *The Thee Generation*, 53–59.

16. Fox, *The Case for Animal Experimentation*, 38.

17. Ibid.

18. Rosemary Rodd, *Biology, Ethics and Animals* (Oxford: Clarendon Press, 1990), 23.

19. Ibid., 34.

20. Fox, *The Case for Animal Experimentation*, 35.

21. Rodd, *Biology, Ethics and Animals*, 82.

22. Ibid., 68.

23. Ibid., 98.

24. Michael W. Fox, "Man and Nature: Biological Perspectives," in Morris and Fox, 124.

25. Rodd, *Biology, Ethics and Animals*, 30–31.

26. Ibid., 31.

27. Ibid., 23.

28. Quoted in Fox, *The Case for Animal Experimentation*, 34.

29. Rodd, *Biology, Ethics and Animals*, 76.

30. Ibid., 77.

31. This is the core of radical behaviorist thought (B. F. Skinner, *About Behaviorism* [New York: Random House, 1974], 10–23).

32. John Robbins, *Diet for a New America* (Walpole, N.H.: Stillpoint, 1987), 32–33.

33. Rodd, *Biology, Ethics and Animals*, 36.

34. Robbins, *Diet for a New America*, 24–25 30.

35. Ibid., 29–30.

36. Ibid., 21–22.

37. Ibid., 29.

38. Fox, *The Case for Animal Experimentation*, 50–59.

39. Dale Jamieson, "Killing Persons and Other Beings," in Miller and Williams, *Ethics and Animals*, 145.

Chapter 3

1. Plato, *The Republic*, bk. II in *Great Dialogues of Plato*, ed. W. H. D. Rouse (New York: The New English Library Ltd., 1956).
2. Quoted in Steven Rosen, *Food for the Spirit: Vegetarianism and the World Religious* (San Diego: Bala/Entourage Books, 1990), 108.
3. Ibid., 109–10.
4. Rosen, *Food for the Spirit*, iii.
5. Richard Leakey and Roger Lewin, *Origins* (New York: Dutton, 1977), 153.
6. Fox, *The Case for Animal Experimentation*, 21.
7. Leakey and Lewin, *Origins*, 153.
8. Amato and Partridge, *The New Vegetarians*, 2.
9. Leakey and Lewin, *Origins*, 150.
10. Rosen, *Food for the Spirit*, 10.
11. Hans Reusch, *Slaughter of the Innocent* (New York: Bantam, 1978), 405–6.
12. From the Preamble of the Constitution of the World Health Organization, reprinted in Tom L. Beauchamp and LeRoy Walters, *Contemporary Issues in Bioethics* (Belmont, California: Wadsworth, 1989), 79.
13. Amato and Partridge, *The New Vegetarians*, 32–34.
14. Ibid. 9.
15. Robbins, *Diet for a New America* 195; Amato and Partridge, *The New Vegetarians*, 6.
16. Robbins, *Diet for a New America*, 300.
17. Ibid., 299.
18. Ibid., 9.
19. Ibid.
20. Robbins, *Diet for a New America*, 300.
21. Amato and Partridge, *The New Vegetarians*, 103–4.
22. Ibid., 104.
23. Ibid., 113.
24. Joy Gross and Karen Freifeld, *The Vegetarian Child* (Secaucus, N.J.: Lyle Stuart Inc., 1983), 37–38.
25. Robbins, *Diet for a New America*, 154.
26. Amato and Partridge, *The New Vegetarians*, 10–12.
27. Robbins, *Diet for a New* America, 215.
28. Amato and Partridge, *The New Vegetarians*, 11–13; Gross and Freifeld, *The Vegetarian Child*, 61–63.
29. Gross and Freifeld, *The Vegetarian Child*, 64–65; also see "Vegetarian Diets," *Journal of the American Dietetic Assoc.* (March, 1988).

30. Rifkin, *Beyond Beef* 166.

31. Gross and Freifeld, *The Vegetarian Child*, 59.

32. Rifkin, *Beyond Beef*, 172.

33. Ibid.

34. Rosen, *Food for the Spirit*, 9.

35. Robbins, *Diet for a New America*, 251.

36. Gross and Freifeld, *The Vegetarian Child*, 52.

37. Jim Mason "Brave New Farm," in Peter Singer, *In Defense of Animals* (New York: Basil Blackwell, 1985), 100.

38. Ibid.

39. Pringle, *The Animal Rights Controversy*, 38.

40. Rifkin, *Beyond Beef*, 12–13.

41. Gross and Freifeld, *The Vegetarian Child*, 50.

42. Mason, "Brave New Farm" 100.

43. Gross and Freifeld, *The Vegetarian Child*, 52.

44. Rifkin, *Beyond Beef*, 13.

45. Pringle, *The Animal Rights Controversy*, 33–34.

46. Robbins, *Diet for a New America*, 67.

47. Rifkin, *Beyond Beef*, 143–44.

48. Ibid.

49. Ibid., 136–37

50. Gross and Freifeld, *The Vegetarian Child*, 146–47.

51. Amato and Partridge, *The New Vegetarians*, 7.

52. Gross and Freifeld, *The Vegetarian Child*, 50.

53. Frances Moore Lappé, *Diet for a Small Planet* (New York: Ballantine, 1982).

54. Rosen, *Food for the Spirit*, 5–7; Gross and Freifeld, *The Vegetarian Child*, 54.

55. Gross and Freifeld *The Vegetarian Child*, 53.

56. Robbins, *Diet for a New America*, 195.

57. Amato and Partridge, *The New Vegetarians*, 6.

58. Robbins, *Diet for a New America*, 189–93.

59. Amato and Partridge, *The New Vegetarians*, 14.

60. Robbins *Diet for a New America*, 189–93.

61. Richard Bergen, M.D., *The Vegetarian's Self-Defense Manual* Wheaton, Ill.: Theosophical Pub., 1979), 60–67; Gross and Freifeld, *The Vegetarian Child*.

62. Jimmy M. Skaggs, *Prime Cut* (College Station, Tex.: A & M University Press, 1976).

63. Harriet Schleifer, "Images of Death and Life: Food Animal Production and the Vegetarian Option," in Singer, *In Defense of Animals*, 67.

64. Skaggs, *Prime Cut*.
65. Rifkin, *Beyond Beef*, 21.
66. Robbins, *Diet for a New America*, 157–58.
67. Ibid., 158–61.
68. Ibid., 158.
69. Ibid., 157–58.
70. Amato and Partridge, *The New Vegetarians*, 116–26.
71. Ibid., 126–29.

Chapter 4

1. Schleifer, "Images of Death and Life" in Singer, *In Defense of Animals*, 68.
2. Rifkin, *Beyond Beef*, 185–91.
3. Ibid., 105–6.
4. Ibid., 125–31.
5. Skaggs, *Prime Cut*.
6. Ibid.
7. Robbins, *Diet for a New America*, 361.
8. Ibid, 360.
9. Rifkin, *Beyond Beef*, 98.
10. Robbins, *Diet for a New America*, 356.
11. Ibid.
12. Rifkin, *Beyond Beef*, 202.
13. Robbins, *Diet for a New America*, 358.
14. Ibid.
15. Ibid., 356.
16. Rifkin, *Beyond Beef*, 217.
17. Ibid., 202.
18. Robbins, *Diet for a New America*, 356.
19. Amato and Partridge, *The New Vegetarians*, 19.
20. Schleifer, "Images of Death and Life," 68.
21. Amato and Partridge, *The New Vegetarians*, 19.
22. Ibid., 22.
23. Schleifer, "Images of Death and Life," 68.
24. Rifkin, *Beyond Beef*, 221.
25. Amato and Partridge, *The New Vegetarians*, 20.
26. Rifkin, *Beyond Beef*, 221.
27. Lewis Regenstein, "Animal Rights, Endangered Species and Human Survival," in Singer, *In Defense of Animals*.
28. Rifkin, *Beyond Beef*, 205.

29. Ibid. 198.

30. Fox, *The Case for Animal Experimentation*, 20.

31. Tom Regan, *All That Dwell Therein: Animal Rights and Environmental Ethics* (Berkeley, California: University of California Press, 1982).

32. Pringle, *The Animal Rights Controversy*, 28.

33. Schleifer, "Images of Death and Life," 68.

34. Dean Edwin Abrahamson, *The Challenge of Global Warming* (Washington, D.C.: Island Press, 1989), 4.

35. Ibid., 6–7.

36. Ibid., xiv.

37. Ibid., 4–5.

38. Ibid., 5.

39. Ibid., 13.

40. Ibid., 76.

41. Ralph J. Cicerone, "Methane in the Atmosphere," in Fred Singer, *Global Climate Changes"* (New York: Paragon, 1989), 102, table 6–2.

42. Cicerone, "Methane in the Atmosphere," 102: Donald R. Blake, "Methane, CFCs and Other Greenhouse Gases," in Abrahamson, *The Challenge of Global Warming*, 348–55.

43. Abahamson, *The Challenge of Global Warming*, 74.

44. Ibid., 12.

45. Rifkin, *Beyond Beef*, 225.

46. Ibid., 217.

47. Richard Knowles Morris, "Man and Animals: Some Contemporary Problems," in Morris and Fox *On the Fifth Day*, 30.

48. James E. Lovelock, "The Evolution of Gaia," in *Greenhouse Glastnost: The Crisis of Global Warming*, ed. Terrece J. Minger (New York: Ecco Press, 1990).

49. Independent Commission on International Human Issues, *Famine: A Man–made Disaster?* (New York, Random House, 1985), 14.

Chapter 5

1. Rifkin, *Beyond Beef*, 282.

2. Schleifer, "Images of Death and Life" in Singer, *In Defense of Animals*, 68.

3. Patricia L. Kutzner, *World Hunger* (Santa Barbara, California: ABC–Clio, 1991), 2.

4. Independent Commission, *Famine: A Man–Made Disaster?* 26.

5. Ibid., 27.

Notes

6. Kutzner, *World Hunger*, 2.

7. Ibid.

8. Independent Commission, *Famine: A Man-Made Disaster?*, 26.

9. See chapter 2 for a discussion of this.

10. Radha Sinha, *Food and Poverty* (London: Croom Helm, 1976), 10–15.

11. Independent Commission, *Famine: A Man-Made Disaster?*, 75–76.

12. Sinha, *Food and Poverty*, 9–10.

13. Kutzner, *World Hunger*, 1.

14. Arthur Simon, *Bread for the World* (New York: Wm. B. Eerdman's Pub. Co., 1984), 19.

15. Independent Commission, *Famine: A Man-Made Disaster?*, 10.

16. Peter Singer, "The Famine Relief Argument," *Morality in Practice* James P. Serba ed. (Belmont, California: Wadsworth, 1984), 82.

17. The classic statement is Robert Nozick, *Anarchy, State and Utopia* (Cambridge, Mass.: Harvard University Press, 1974).

18. Singer, "The Famine Relief Argument."

19. Frances Moore Lappé and Joseph Collins, *World Hunger: Twelve Myths* (New York: Grove Weidenfeld, 1986), 9–14.

20. Ibid., 25–26.

21. Rifkin, *Beyond Beef*, 59.

22. Amato and Partridge, *The New Vegetarians*, 19.

23. Rosen, *Food for the Spirit*, 7–8.

24. Amato and Partridge, *The New Vegetarians*, 21.

25. Rifkin, *Beyond Beef*, 60–61.

26. Amato and Partridge, *The New Vegetarians*, 21.

27. Rifkin, *Beyond Beef*, 161.

28. Rosen, *Food for the Spirit*, 7.

29. See chapter 4 for a discussion of this.

30. Independent Commission, *Famine: A Man-Made Disaster?*, 75.

31. Ibid., 75–6.

32. Lappé and Collins, *World Hunger: Twelve Myths*, 9.

33. Simon, *Bread for the World*, 18.

34. Kutzner, *World Hunger*, 1.

35. Independent Commission, *Famine: A Man-Made Disaster?*, 23–46.

36. Ibid., 81.

37. Ibid., 54–55.

38. Ibid., 90–100.

39. Rifkin, *Beyond Beef*, 92–99.

40. Ibid., 213.

Chapter 6

1. James Cargile, "Comments on The Priority of Human Interests," in Harlan B. Miller and William H. Williams, ed. *Ethics and Animals* (Clifton, N.J.: Humana Press, 1983), 249.

2. Jan Narveson, "Animal Rights Revisited" in Miller and Williams, *Ethics and Animals* 50–51.

3. Quoted in Cargile, "Comments on `The Priority of Human Interests,'" 249.

4. This, of course, is a fundamentally deontological response to the Argument from Nonexistence.

5. See chapter 4 for a discussion.

6. Amato and Partridge, *The New Vegetarians*: 98.

7. Interestingly, I found that a surprisingly large number of my colleagues were stealth vegetarians.

8. Quoted in Ashley Montagu, "Is Man Innately Aggressive?" in Morris and Fox, *On the Fifth Day: Animal Rights and Human Ethics*, 97–98.

9. Fox, *The Case for Animal Experimentation* 35.

10. Alfie Kohn, *The Brighter Side of Human Nature* (New York: Basic Books, 1990).

11. F. S. C. Northrop, "Naturalistic Realism and Animate Compassions," in Morris and Fox, *On the Fifth Day*.

12. James Rachels, "Active and Passive Euthanasia," in *Morality and Moral Controversies*, John Arthur ed., (Englewood Cliffs, N.J., 1986).

13. Fox, *The Case for Animal Experimentation*.

14. T. Nicholaus Tideman, "Deciding What To Kill," in Miller and Williams, *Ethics and Animals*.

15. Rodd, *Biology, Ethics and Animals*, 26–30.

16. Regan, *The Case for Animal Rights*.

17. Rifkin, *Beyond Beef*, 125.

18. Ibid., 131.

19. Ibid., 127–28.

20. Ibid. 128.

21. Ibid., 127.

22. Ibid., 105–6.

23. Fox, *The Case for Animal Experimentation*, 15.

24. Amato and Partridge, *The New Vegetarians*, 203.

25. Schleifer, "Images of Death and Life" in Singer, *In Defense of Animals,* 72–73.

Chapter 7

1. Amato and Partridge, *The New Vegetarians* 1.
2. Ibid., 32–34.
3. Carol J. Adams, *The Sexual Politics of Meat: A Feminist Vegetarian Critical Theory* (New York: Continuum, 1990).
4. Quoted in Amy Freeman Lee, "A Game for All Seasons," in Morris and Fox, *On the Fifth Day.*
5. Crane Brinton, *A History of Western Morals* (New York: Harcourt Brace, 1959).
6. Quoted in Schleifer, "Images of Life and Death" in Singer, *In Defense of Animals.*
7. Henry David Thoreau, *Walden* (New York: Viking Penguin, 1985).

Index

animals: as moral agents, 62–65; extermination of, statistics, 48

animals and humans: behavioral similarities, 55–62; brain structure, 53–54; genetic similarities, 54–55

animal intelligence and awareness, 37–39, 45–46, 52–62

animal rights, 40–52

Aquinas, St. Thomas, 35, 72

Argument from Inconvenience, the, 154–57

Argument from Innate Human Aggression, the, 157–61

Argument from Nonexistence, the, 150–53

Aristotle, 1, 7, 10–12, 71, 76, 101

athletes and vegetarianism, 95–98

Augustine, St., 35, 72, 123

Benedict, St., x, 34

Bentham, Jeremy, 8, 13, 15 19, 65

Buddhism, 32–33

Camus, Albert, 167

cancer. See meat eating and cancer

Cargile, James, 150

children and vegetarianism, 94–95

Christian attitudes to vegetarianism, 32–37, 72, 123–26 consciousness as a moral criterion, 65–67

Constantine, 34, 72

Crysothum, St. John, 34

cultural relativism, 4–7, 25, 178–81

Cyprian, 34

Dart, Raymond, 158

deforestation and desertification, 107–10, 115, 121–22

deontology, 8–10, 19–23, 28; objections to, 21–23; and vegetarianism, 46–52, 165; and world hunger, 135–36. See also animal rights

Descartes, 38

destruction of other species, 114–19

Diogenes the Cynic, 1

displacement of population, 122, 145

ecology. See global ecology

Edison, Thomas, x

egoism, ethical, 102–3

Einstein, Albert, 69, 186

emotivism, ethical, 3–4

Eusebius, 34

experimentation on animals: statistics, vii–viii, 37–39

factory farms, 41–43

fallacy of black and white thinking, the, 165–69

famine. See world hunger

197

About the Author

John Lawrence Hill received a J.D. and a Ph.D. in philosophy from Georgetown University. He has taught logic, moral philosophy, and general philosophy courses at a number of universities throughout the United States. He is currently associate professor of law at St. Thomas University, School of Law in Miami, Florida. Professor Hill teaches constitutional law, jurisprudence, and ethics courses at the law school. He has been a vegetarian since 1983.